God's Girls

Ordination of Women in the Early Christian & Gnostic Churches

Arthur Frederick Ide

Garland
Tangelwüld
1986

Published by
Tangelwüld Press
P.O. Box 475961
Garland, Texas 75047-5961

© **Arthur Frederick Ide, 1985**

Library of Congress Cataloging-in-Publication Data

Ide, Arthur Frederick.
  God's girls.

  Bibliography: p.
  Includes index.
  1. Ordination of women - - History. 2. Women in the
Bible. 3. Jesus Christ - - Views on women. 4. Women in
Christianity - - History. I. Title.
BV676.I33 1986   262'.1411   85-27808
ISBN 0-934667-01-2 (pbk.)

For

Sandra Wilson
Rockford, Michigan

Whose faith in God
Love for the Reformed Church of Jesus Christ Latter Day Saints
Devotion to Knowledge
Stalwart Friendship
and
Unparalleled Spirit
Inspires Others
To Climb Mountains Some Area Afraid to Approach

TABLE OF CONTENTS

Introduction

Historically women have been discriminated against. Not only have women been denied equality before the law, but equal justice in the home, the market, and in the rites and officiations of religion.

Nowhere has woman suffered more than in the evolution of the Christian church. From the fifth century to the present, misogynistic ministers and chauvinistic clerics have pontificated from pulpits of stone, wood, and natural formations that woman is inferior, that woman is to be subject to the man, and that in matters of faith she is to be silent. Their words have been accepted for a variety of reasons by not only the men who listened to them, but pathetically by the women themselves who had a long and glorious record of caring for the souls and tending to the physical bodily needs of food, shelter and comfort since the days of Christ when Martha prepared his supper and Mary learned at his feet.

The rank ignorance of Richard Land of First Baptist Church of Dallas' Criswell Center for Biblical Studies in preaching that "Timothy" rejected women as co-equal with men in spreading the faith has opiated many minds and heralded the possibility of an impending Dark Age in the story of civilization if his comments remain unchallenged. Yet, even though Richard Land argues on and for the literal interpretation of the English bible as the foundation for his anti-woman stand, his bibliolatry is concurred with both actively and passively by numerous

Fundamentalist theologians—both Protestant and Catholic (Roman, Greek, and other)—who have, especially in America elevated the British sovereign who convened a gathering of English teaching preachers to meet at Hampton Court in 1611, King James to near hagiographic laudations as "Saint James." Not only did this interesting ruler who deeply loved George Villiers, the Duke of Buckingham (who was affectionately called "Stinky") create a masterpiece of English prose—albeit mediocre to down-right poor theology both in theology and in presentation at publication—but he generated a new cult of idol worship—the literalizing of scripture by those whose linquistic and exegetical prowess prove weak to non-existent.

Yet women have been priests and bishops in the very churches which deny that they ever functioned in a sacerdotal manner. Instead, at best a few of the Fundamentalist churches acknowledge that the United Church of Christ did ordain women as early as 1853, but discount the ordinations since that church in the nineteenth century appeared to cater only to misfits, the poor, and the "untouchables" in American society. A few churches, and some rabbinical centers and synagogues today, in the late twentieth century, admit women to ordination, and a rare brave few, such as the United Methodist Church anoint an occasional woman as bishop (two of the 46 bishops of the United Methodist Church are women, while another woman, Marjorie Suchocki, is dean of Wesley Theological Seminary in Washington, D.C.). Other denominations, especially the Roman Catholic church, continue to degrade women by rejecting their

Christ-given right to be priests and bishops—even when some women, such as Sister Dorothy Feehan, who helps to administer the 290-family Spirit of Peace Catholic Community in Longmont, Colorado, have enough theological credits to qualify as priests. Yet these women are eager to serve, actively involved in church ministrations on lower levels, and frequently more competent and better versed than their male counterparts who are ordained and forbid them to enter the same mission which was first announced to a woman—Mary—who in turn relayed it to doubting men who were not as ready nor as eager to "go forth to all nations, baptizing and preaching in" the name of Jesus. These men are still bound by the biased perspective that the male is the norm and good while the female is the inferior and evil—a concept fostered and furthered by a continuing depreciation and misinterpretation of the Creation Narrative.[1]

Anxious to serve, the number of female seminarians skyrocketed from 3,558 in 1972 to 13,451 in 1983. At the same time their share of total enrollment jumped from 10.2% to 24.4%, their commitment more outspoken and visibily demonstrated, their charity and compassion more universal and genuine, and their studies more diligent and fervent than their male counterparts. Rebecca Chopp of the University of Chicago Divinity School predicted in 1984 that by the year 2000, the majority of the seminarians will be women, and in turn it will be women who will fill the number of clerical appointments as men continue to seek other careers. Yet if this is to be a reality, and churches do not go for want of ministers, it will take men of quality who are not threatened by women seeking equality, to appoint qualified and capable women to vacancies.[2]

The Southern Baptist Convention is in the lead of those denominations putting baskets over candles, denying women their Christian right to preach and teach as ministers of Jesus. In the summer of 1984 "messengers" to the 14-million member Southern Baptist Convention approved a resolution railroaded through by Richard Land and other misogynists of the Criswell Center for Biblical Studies opposing the ordination of women—even though, ludicrous as it is, over 300 Southern Baptist women have already been ordained, and their number is increasing by no less than one a week. Ordination, however, is not appointment, as Peg Witt of Durham, North Carolina found out, for although she was ordained in March 1984, she is still seeking a job.

As the bigotry of the radical right lunatic fringe continues to suffocate the Southern Baptist church, women who are devoted to their god and their denomination are reluctant to wait. Some, in fact, have renounced their Southern Baptist heritage, broken with the cadaver of their church now enchained by the strict literalists, and have adopted similar confessions and accepted ordination in other churches—especially in the United Methodist movement.[3] Others, such as Sandra Mills, a graduating theological student at Southwestern Baptist Theological Seminary in Fort Worth, Texas, have decided on alternative careers— unwilling to fight the tyranny of Richard Land and

men of his persuasion who preach against women in the
ministry—yet who, like Falwell, use women to interpret
their messages of hate and bigotry to the hearing dis-
abled—never once realizing that those women talented
in sign languages for the hearing impaired are in that
capacity acting as ministers of the very word they are
forbidden to preach.

The greatest bigotry, however, does not come from
the strict Fundamentalist movement, but instead from the
Roman Catholic Church. Ignoring not only Scripture, but
tradition as well, twentieth century bishops in insipid
ignorance of the past glory of women in the priesthood,
to which they were called, commissioned and ordained
have been denied their right to fulfill their calling. Instead of acknowledging the historic right of women to
be priests, the Roman Catholic heirarchy, led by the
myopic mentality of John Paul II, have been relegated
to the dung-heaps of their zombie-like minds which
painfully justify woman's existence on earth by "allowing women" select "pastoral duties" in the priest-short
parishes *provided* that they do not ask nor attempt to
administer the sacraments.

Like other irrational acts of gynophobic men, the
male heirarcy in the Roman Catholic Church delights in
abusing women's minds in a childish manner by proclaiming that women are "good as nuns, reserved for the Lord
[Jesus Christ]"—especially when "at their prayers and
penances"—but not equal to man, and thereby not "good
enough for the Lord" to lead the church in its fulfillment
of prayers by administering the sacraments. Yet Christ

told women to "go forth and preach to all nations"—a message *not* reserved for men, being given first to a woman.

The problem is in the minds of men. But the solution is in the power of women.

Not until women band together in pursuit of equality and justice will they realize their natural right to function in whatever calling, job, vocation, or service they desire. Not until women band together to insist on equality, will women be treated equally.

The solution is simple: women must refuse to attend the services of gynophobic, disabling, xenophobic, mysogynistic male ministers until their boycott effects the necessary revolution and women are allowed to join them in full partnership preaching the message that they feel inside of them. If women boycott the churches and synogogues across the nation and the world which denies them their rights to the priesthood many more generations will pass before their heirs will see the opportunity they long for. Until women refuse to accept sacramentals and participate in any number of sacraments when administered by men who deny women's equality, women will never be able to administer those very same sacraments. This is not to say that women must boycott all churches and synogogues nor refuse the sacraments from all male clergy—it is only to affirm that the beginning of the dignity of woman will come when woman rejects the chauvinism preached and enforced by men who deny woman the right to equality, equal access to the pulpit and altar, and reject their participation in the church rites and rituals on par with themselves. A revolution of determined silence and the willingness to give up temporary pleasures and peace in justified rebellion to obtain freedom is not only good but correct behavior.

The necessary revolution however cannot be fought only with silence and abstention. It must also include an economic boycott of the churches and synagogues which preach, like Richard Land of Dallas, the theme of the inequality of women before god. This economic boycott must include a discontinuation of monetary contributions not only for the upkeep of the edifice which houses the bigots parading in clerical garments, but it must be the withdrawal of funds from all church related activities: missions, schools, and the like. No boycott is effective that is a partial boycott, for shrewd financial administrators are able to juggle existing funding to meet the most pressing demands of the moment—which generally is the maintenance of the employment of the bigots who preach against women. Furthermore, it stands to reason, this economic boycott must extend into the schools of the churches which preach against women, by conscientious women who yearn to be free and equal to man in the standing of the church, withdrawing their children from the parochial school, by resigning from committees and study groups, and by the establishment of their own seminaries and ultimately their own congregations. When this occurs the revolution becomes a reformation—long overdo, equal not only to the message hammered on the door of Wittenburg church by the radical monk Martin Luther, but demonstrated in this generation in St. Louis, Missouri, when Seminex was founded by the Lutherans of the Missouri Synod who could no longer tolerate the capricious control of thought by the staid and ossified who are determined to inquisitorially "weed-out" and suffocate any thought or expression which does not agree with their own.

Historically religions have never been passive. Instead, most religious movements have been revolutionary, icon-oclastic, determinedly independent and quick to take in the disenfranchised.[4] Christianity today, however, has fallen into the opiate of contentment with the status quo—ranging from religious opposition to fundamental rights to Jerry Falwell's rank racist bigotry and condemnation of the freedom movement in apartheid-controlled Union of South Africa while he continues to preach pleadingly for more and more money.

Jesus was a revolutionary. There was nothing passive in him or his message. He not only kicked money-changers out of the Temple, but called women to his side as equals, allowing them to sit at his feet in study and conversation. If women are truly called to him, they must become like him and lead America to a new revolution.

NOTES

[1] See my *Teachings of Jesus on Women* (Dallas: TIP, 1984).

[2] "Women of the Cloth: How They're Faring," *U.S. News & World Report* (3 December 1984) pp. 76-77.

[3] *Ibid.*, pp. 77. See also my *Unholy Rollers: the Selling of Jesus* (Arlington: Liberal Arts, 1985), and my *Demons & Demigogues: Political Fanaticism in the Longhorn State* (Las Colinas: The Liberal Press, 1985). Cp. my *Woman as Priest, Bishop & Laity* (Mesquite: Ide House, 1984), and my *Sex, Woman & Religion* (Dallas: Monument Press, 1984).

[4] See my *Martyrdom of Women : A Study of Death Psychology in the Early Christian Church to 301 CE* (Garland: Tangelwüld, 1985).

Chapter One
Jesus & Women

Jesus affirmed the equality of the sexes. Disavowing the Jewish law which only permitted men to instigate divorce (Deut. 24:1; cp. Ben Sira 25:23-26, and, Mishnah 9, 10), Jesus acknowledged women's right to divorce (Mk. 10:12). At the same time, it must be noted, Jesus also addressed equal responsibilities to women (Mk. 10:2-12; Matt. 19:3-6), which had to be accepted if women were to share in the benefits previously accorded only to men (Matt. 22:23-30, cf. Mk. 12:18-27; Lk. 20:27-38).

Women were help*mates*, so the man of Galilee argued. Women were not servants (Mk. 1:41; Lk. 7:14, 13:10-17).

Jesus had no fear of women. Women were not vile and corrupting, as so many of his contemporaries argued heatedly. Women had value, purpose, dignity, rights—on par with men (Lk. 13:12).[1]

Jesus' attitude towards women can be seen in his attitude towards his mother. Whereas most Jewish sons gave rather mediocre filial respect to their mothers, Jesus was, in every recorded instance, fully respectful to her. This is not to say that his life with Mary was one of constant and continuing bliss. There were disagreements, and misunderstandings: καὶ εἶπε πρὸς αὐτύς Τί ὅτι ἐξητεῖτέ με (Lk. 2:49, yet which he still yielded on: οὐκ ᾔδειτε ὅτι ἐν τοῖς τοῦ πατρός μου δεῖ εἶναί με καὶ αὐτοὶ οὐ συνῆκαν τὸ ῥῆμα ὃ ἐλάλησεν αὐτοῖς (Lk. 2:50-51).[2] (Although this reply is considered to be an admonition to his mother, the text does not support this; a reading should be: *Why did you* [pl.] *seek me out; did you not know that it is morally necessary* [dei] *for me to be about the affairs of my Father?*). In this regard, Jesus elevated his vocation above his familial responsibilities and affections. This, in turn, brough out quite clearly his enigmatic question, "What [is their between] me and you [*Ti emoi kai soi* (Τί ἐμοὶ καὶ σοί)]" (Jn 2:4).

The comment Jesus made, following his original ques-

tion addressed to his parents in the temple (*Ti emoi kai soi*), demonstrates that Jesus considered his mission of spreading the peace he felt was instilled within him was of greater importance and urgency than the customary honor and respect (or filial piety) society expected him to offer to his mother or his father—even if, by doing so, it led to a rupture in their relationship. This rupture, however, never occurred, for Mary appears in the text to be a woman of great compassion, understanding—especially after the Magnificat—and love. She accepted the injunction of her son, eventhough there is no indication in the text that she understood the impact or import of that message. One thing is clear in all the readings is that neither the mother (Mary), nor the son (Jesus) abandoned the other at that time—or later. (Jn. 19:25-27). Instead, we need only read a little further to see that Jesus affirmed his parents and parenthood in general. Luke notes, unequivocably, that Jesus "lived under the authority" of his mother and father (Lk. 2:51). At the same time Jesus, unlike his contemporaries, did not set his father (Joseph) above his mother. Instead, Jesus saw both of his parents as equals to one another in all respects:

Pharisees and scribes from Jerusalem then came to Jesus and said, "Why do your disciples break away from the tradition of the elders? They do not wash their hands when they eat food." "And why do you," he answered, "break away from the command-ment of God for the sake of your tradition? For God said: Do your duty to your father and mother, and: Any-one who curses father or mother must be put to death. But you say, 'If anyone says to his father or mother: Any-thing I have that I might have used to help you is

Τότε προσέρχονται τῶ Ἰησοῦ ἀπὸ Ἰεροσολύμων Φαρισαῖοι καὶ γραμματεῖς λέγοντες Διατί οἱ μαθηταί σου παραβαίνουσι τήν παράδοσιν τῶν πρεσβυτ-έρων οὐ γὰρ νίπτονται τὰς χεῖρας ὅταν ἄρτον ἐσθίωσιν ὁ δὲ ἀποκριθεὶς εἶπεν αὐτοῖς Διατί καὶ ὑμεῖς παραβαίνετε τὴν ἐντολὴν τοῦ Θεοῦ διὰ τὴν παράδοσιν ὑμῶν ὁ γὰρ Θεὸς εἶπε Τίμα τὸν πατέρα καὶ τὴν μητέρα καί Ὁ κακολογῶν πατέρα ἢ μητέρα θανάτω τελευτάτω· ὑμεῖς δὲ λέγετε Ὃς ἂν εἴπῃ τῶ πατρὶ ἢ τῆ μητρί Δῶρον ὃ ἐὰν ἐξ ἐμοῦ ὠφεληθῆς οὐ μὴ τιμήσει τὸν πατέρα αὐτοῦ· καὶ ἠκυρώσατε

dedicated to God,' he is rid of his duty to father or mother. In this way you have made God's work null and void by means of your tradition.   Hypocrites!"

τὸν λόγον τοῦ Θεοῦ, διὰ τὴν παράδοσιν ὑμῶν, ὑποκριταί καλῶς προεφήτευσε περὶ ὑμῶν Ἡσαΐας

(Matt. 15:7)

Jesus did not have an untroubled childhood. His parents had strong questions concerning his sanity, for he was an independent thinker—whose thoughts and actions were outside of the mainstream of his civilization, bringing to his society discontent and disquiet. His society, in turn, reacted against the boy and rejected him and his family. In this acute situtation, his parents attempted to protect him, barring the community in which they lived away from him:

He went home once more, and once more such a large crowd gathered that they could not eat a meal. When his family heard of this, they set out to take charge of him, convinced that he was no longer of sound mind.

Και ερχ εις οικον° και συνερχεται πελιν ο οχλος ωστε μη δυνασθαι αυτονς μηδε αρτον φαγειν° και ακουσαντες οι παρ αυτου εξηγθον κρατησαι αυτον°...

Because of this incident, and similar incidents (cf. Matt. 13:53-58; Mk. 6:1-6; Lk. 4:16-30), Jesus remarked, *"A prophet is only despised in his own country, among his own relations, and in his own house." (Mk. 6:5-6).* Undoubtedly it was this social confrontation which made Jesus keenly aware of what could constitute his family: be it the primary circle or some periphery. In the end, he chose to call those who loved him and needed him, seeking him out for healing, ministry, and love, his family:

He was still speaking to the crowds when his mother and his brethren appeared; they were standing outside and were anxious to have a word with him

Ἔτι αὐτοῦ λαλοῦντος τοῖς ὄχλοις ἰδοὺ ἡ μήτηρ καὶ οἱ ἀδελφοὶ εἰστήκεισαν ἔξω ζητοῦντες αὐτῷ λαλῆσαι· εἶπε δέ τις αὐτῷ Ἰδοὺ ἡ μήτηρ σου καὶ οἱ

But to the man who told him this, Jesus replied, "Who is my mother? Who are my relatives?" And stretching out his hand towards his disciples he said, "Here are my mother and my brothers. Anyone who does the will of my Father in heaven, he is my brother and sister and mother."

ἀδελφοί σου ἔξω ἐστήκασι ζητοῦντές σοι λαλῆσαι· ὁ δὲ ἀποκριφεὶς εἶπε τῷ εἰπόντι αὐτῷ Τίς ἐστιν ἡ μήτηρ μου καὶ τίνες εἰσὶν οἱ ἀδελφοί μου καὶ ἐκτείνας τὴν χεῖρα αὐτοῦ ἐπὶ τοὺς μαθητὰς αὐτοῦ εἶπεν, Ἰδού ἡ μήτηρ μου καὶ οἱ ἀδελφοί μου· ὅστις γὰρ ἂν ποιήσῃ τὸ θέλημα τοῦ πατρός μου ἐν οὐρανοῖς αὐτός μου ἀδελφὸς καὶ ἀδελφὴ καὶ μήτηρ ἐστίν

(Matt. 12:46-50; cf. Mk. 3:31-35; Lk. 8:19-21, and 11:27-28).

The choreography of Jesus' seeming estrangement from his family appears in even later texts (Matt. 10:28-38, and 19:29, Lk. 12:51-53, 14:26, and 18:28-30), but in each case it is not the absolute rejection of his family, but the increased broadening of the base of that family he would recognize and remember. Part of the reason for Jesus' broadening the base of his family was because his own "brothers" had doubts about his sanity and "mission" on earth (Jn. 19:25-27); but this "rejection" was overcome by calling for new "brothers" (Jn. 7:5; Lk. 8:21).[2] This new "family" would be more than a terrestrial family (Matt. 3:8; Lk. 3:8, 16:13; Jn. 8:39), for it would be all encompassing. Furthermore, it shows implicitly and explicitly that Jesus was not bound by sexual qualifiers, distinctions or determinates: he accepted both men and women on an equal basis (Lk. 8:1-3).[3] His invitation was open to all *humankind*—provided that each member of the *human race* was equally open to accept all others. We see it best in the confrontation Jesus experienced with the Syrophoenician woman who persisted in getting near him, demanded healing, and then bested Jesus in a verbal exchange—she was definitely *not* an inferior.

Jesus left that place and withdrew to the region of Tyre and Sidon. Then out came a Canaan-

Καὶ ἐξελθὼν ἐκεῖθεν ὁ Ἰησοῦς ἀνεχώρησεν εἰς τὰ μέρη Τύρου καὶ Σιδῶνος· καὶ ἰδού γυνὴ

ite woman from that district and [she] started shouting, "Sir, Son of David, take pity on me. My daughter is tormented by a devil." But he answered her not a word. And his disciples went and pleaded with him, "Give her what she wants," they said. "Because she is shouting after us." He said in reply, "I was sent only to the lost sheep of the House of Israel." But the woman had come up and was kneeling at his feet. "Lord," she said, "help me." He replied, "It is not fit to take the children's food and throw it to the house-dogs." She retorted, "Ah, yes, sir, but even house-dogs can eat the scraps from their master's table." Then Jesus answered her, "Woman, you have great faith. Let your wish be granted." And from that moment her daughter was well again."

Χαναναία ἀπὸ τῶν ὁρίωο ἐκείνω εκεωων ἐξελθοῦσα ἐκραύγασε λέγουσα Ἐλέησόν με Κύριε υἱέ Δαβίδ∘ ἡ θυγάτηρ μου κακῶς δαιμονίζεται∘ ο δὲ οὐκ ἀπεκρίθη αὐτῇ λόγον∘ καὶ προσελθόντες οἱ μαθηταὶ αὐτοῦ ἠρώτων αὐτὸν λέγοντες Ἀπόλυσον αὐτήν ὅτι κράζει ὄπισθεν ἡμῶν∘ ὁ δὲ ἀποκριθεὶς εἶπεν Οὐκ ἀπεστάλην εἰ μὴ εἰς τὰ πρόβατα τὰ ἀπολωλότα οἴκου Ισραηλ∙ ἡ δὲ ἐλθοῦσα προσεκύνει αὐτῷ λέγουσα Κύριε βοήθει μοι∙ ὁ δέ ἀποκριθεὶς εἶπεν Οὐκ ἔστι καλὸν λαβεῖν του ἄρτον τῶν τέκνων καὶ βαλεῖν τοῖς κυνερίοις∙ ἡ δὲ εἶπε Ναί Κύριε∘ καὶ γὰρ τὰ κυνάρια ἐσθίει ἀπὸ τῶν ψιχίων τῶν πιπτόντων ἀπὸ τῆς τραπέζης τῶν κυρίων αὐτῶν∙ τότε ἀποκριθεὶς ὁ Ιησοῦς εἶπεν αὐτῇ Ὦ γύναι μεγάλη σου ἡ πίστις∙ γενηθήτω σοι ὡς θέλεις∙ καὶ ἰάθη ἡ θυγάτηρ αὐτῆς ἀπο τῆς ὥρας ἐκείνης∙

(Matt. 15:21-28).[4]

Jesus not only talked with, and disputed with women, but allowed women to minister to his needs:[5]

There were some women watching from a distance. Among them were Mary of Magdala, [and] Mary who was the mother of James the younger and Joset, and Salome. These used to follow him and minister [diekonoun] to him when he was in Galilee.[6] And there were many other women there who had come up to Jerusalem with him.

ἦσαν δὲ καὶ γυναῖκες ἀπὸ μακρόθεν θεωροῦσαι ἐν αἷς καὶ Μαρία ἡ Μαγδαληνῇ καὶ Μαρία ἡ τοῦ Ἰακώβου τοῦ μικροῦ καὶ Ἰωσῆ μήτηρ καὶ Σαλώμη αἱ ὅτε ἦν τῇ Γαλιλαίᾳ ἠκολοβθουν αὐτῷ καὶ διηκόνουν αὐτῷ καὶ ἄλλαι πολλαὶ αἱ συναναβᾶσαι αὐτῷ εἰς Ἱεροσόλυμα∙

(Mk. 15:40-41), which is strengthened by:

And many women were there, watching from a distance, the same women who had followed him from Galilee and ministered [*diakonousai*] to him. Among them were Mary of Magdala, Mary the Mother of James and Joseph, and [Mary] the mother of Zebedee's sons.

ἦσαν δὲ ἐκεῖ γυναῖκες πολλαὶ ἀπὸ μακρόθεν θεωροῦσαι αἵτινες ἠκολούθησαν τῷ Ἰησοῦ ἀπὸ τῆς Γαλιλαίας διακονοῦσαι αὐτῷ· ἐν αἷς ἦν Μαρία ἡ Μαγδαληνὴ καὶ Μαρία ἡ τοῦ Ἰακώβου καὶ Ἰωσῆ μήτηρ καὶ ἡ μήτηρ τῶν υἱῶν Ζεβεδαίου·

(Matt. 27:55-56)

Luke 10:1 argues for seventy disciples—not the traditional "twelve" (which is the number of apostles, accepted by most Biblical interpreters), many of which had to have been women—not only on the basis of the texts cited above, but also as accounted for in the *New Testament Apocrypha*.[7] The argument that women did not work with Jesus is unfounded; much of that argument stemming from male translated accounts of the scriptures, and especially of the account of Christ's banquets with his "followers". The most common argument is around a badly but frequently used translation of the account of the supper at Bethany, where Mary of Magdala anointed Jesus (Matt. 26:6-13; Mk. 14:3-9; Jn. 12:1-8). Although John's account is the only account which talks of Mary "serving" at the banquet, the term he uses in his account is *diekonei*: which is here to be read as "ministered" as one who is equal among equals. No where in the account does Christ rebuke Mary for being present; in fact, none of the male Apostles who were present rebuked her for being there (although women did not eat with men when guests were present, according to the custom and tradition of the day). Therefore, she obviously did not intrude into this male sanctum. The only logical explanation for this fact is to conclude that Mary was an intregal part of the banquet, equal to all of the men (and possibly other women?) present. The only rebuke which appears comes from the man who worried about the "waste" of the ointment— Judas, the Keeper of the Common Purse:

Six days before the Passover, Jesus went to Bethany, where Lazarus was, whom he had raised from the dead. They gave a dinner for him there, Martha waited on them and Lazarus was among those at table. Mary brought in a pound of very costly ointment, pure nard, and with it anointed the feet of Jesus, wiping them with her hair; the house was full of the scent of the ointment. Then Judas Iscariot—one of the disciples, the man who was to betray him—said, "Why wasn't this ointment sold for three hundred denarii, and the money given to the poor?" He said this, not because he cared about the poor, but because he was a thief; he was in charge of the common fund and used to help himself to the contributions. So Jesus said, "Leave her alone; she had to keep this scent for the day of my burial. You have the poor with you always, you will not always have me."

Ὁ οὖν Ἰησοῦς πρὸ ἓξ ἡμερῶν τοῦ πάσχα ἦλθεν εἰς Βηθανίαν ὅπου ἦν Λάζαρος ὅν ἤγειρεν ἐκ νεκρῶν Ἰησοῦς ᵒ ἐποίησαν οὖν αὐτῷ δεῖπνον ἐκεῖᵒ καὶ ἡ Μάρθα διηκόνει ὁ δὲ Λάζαρος εἷς ἦν ἐκ τῶν ἀνακειμένων σὺν αυτῷ· ἡ οὖν Μαρία λαβοῦσα λίτραν μύρου νάρδου πιστικῆς πολυτίμου ἤλειψε τοὺς πόδας τοῦ Ἰησοῦ καὶ ἐξέμαξε ταῖς θριξὶν αὐτῆς τοὺς πόδας αὐτοῦ· ἡ δὲ οἰκία ἐπληρώθη ἐκ τῆς ὀσμῆς του μύρου· λέγει δὲ Ἰούδας ὁ Ἰσκαριώτης εἷς τῶν μαθητῶν αὐτου ὁ μέλλων αὐτὸν παραδιδόναι Διατί τοῦτο τὸ μύρον οὐκ ἐπράθη τριακοσίων δηναρίων καὶ ἐδόθη πτωχοῖς εἶπε δὲ τοῦτο οὐχ ὅτι περὶ τῶν πτωχῶν ἔμελεν αὐτῷ ἀλλ᾽ ὅτι κλέπτης ἦν καὶ τὸ γλωσσόκομον ἔχων τὰ βαλλόμενα ἐβάσταζενᵒ εἶπεν οὖν ὁ Ἰησοῦς Ἄφες αὐτὴν ἵνα εἰς τὴν ἡμέραν τοῦ ἐνταφιασμοῦ μου τηρήσῃ αὐτὸ· τοὺς πτωχοὺς γὰρ πάντοτε ἔχετε μεθ᾽ ἑαυτῶν ἐμὲ δὲ οὐ πάντοτο ἔχετε·

(Jn. 12:1-8).

This passage demonstrates (1) that more than one woman (i.e. Mary and Martha, at least) was there; (2) that the presence of women was not decried; (3) that Martha was a minister to Christ (και η Μαρθα διηκονξι); (4) and, in prophecy of his impending death (thus affirming the fact that women were accepted and acknowledged as prophets and capable of prophecy), Mary served as a prophet (which was a mark of a minister); (5) that Jesus did not rebuke her, nor (6) did any of the apostles with the exception of Judas who was acknowledged to be a thief by one of his own group; and, (7) that the focal point was the anointing, and (8) that was done by a woman. Furthermore, and in line with the custom of the day, (9) it is an acknowledgement, albeit tacit, that it will be at least one woman who will take care of his remains following his death.

The Apostolate of Christ was composed of a number of men—and at least one woman. The term or word "apostle" means, literally, "one sent." Jesus sent (*apostellein*) Mary of Magdala to the male apostles in witness of his resurrection (Jn. 20:17-18: λέγει αὐτῇ ὁ Ἰησοῦς Μή μου ἅπτου οὔπω γὰρ ἀναβέβηκα πρὸς τὸν πατέρα· πορεύου δὲ πρὸς τοὺς ἀδελφούς μου καὶ εἰπὲ αὐτοῖς Ἀναβαίνω πρὸς τὸν πατέρα μου καὶ παι πατέρα ὑμῶν καὶ Θεόν μου καὶ Θεὸν ὑμῶν· ἔρχεται Μαρία ἡ Μαγδαληνὴ ἀγγέλλουσα τοῖς μαθηταῖς ὅτι Ἑώρακα τὸν Κύριον καὶ ταῦτα εἶπεν αὐτῇ). That Jesus commissioned her to be an apostle was well known throughout the early Church through the twelfth century[8]; it was even acknowledged by Bernard of Clairvaux, who refers to her as the "apostle to the apostles."

The apostleship of women is hinted at in the Gospels. All of the writers acknowledge the unique role women played in Christ's final days. All record that only women remained by Jesus through his death on the cross (Matt. 27:55-56; Mk. 15:40-41; Lk. 23:49; Jn. 19:25). All but John acknowledges that women witnessed the burial of Jesus (Matt. 27:61; Mk. 15:47; Lk. 23:55). And all four writers declare that women were the first witnesses to find the empty tomb (Matt. 28:1-8; Mk. 16:1-8; Lk. 24: 1-8; Jn. 20:1-10), while all but Luke (who remains silent on this point) declares that Christ appears to women first after his resurrection (Matt. 28:9-10; Mk. 16:9; Jn. 20:11-17), while all affirm that women were the first to testify about the resurrection to the male disciples and then went out to the community as a whole (Matt. 28:8; Mk. 16:7, 11; Lk. 24:9-11; Jn. 20:18).

NOTES

[1] Mk. 1:41; Lk. 7:14, 13:10-17. Cf. David Daube, "Jesus and the Samaritan Woman: the Meaning of *sugchraomai*," in *Journal of Biblical Literature* 69 no. 2 (June, 1950) pp. 137-147.

[2] The question of whether or not Jesus had biological brothers and sisters remains heatedly debated. The traditional view is that Jesus was the *only* child born to Mary; emerging arguments hold that Jesus was the *first* born of Mary, while some contend that Jesus was the only child born to the *virgin* Mary, and that after his birth, he was succeeded by other siblings either generated by Joseph, or by another husband once Joseph died. The New Testament does not clarify this point; the Gospel writers only declare that Christ had an unspecified number of brothers and sisters (Matt. 12:46-50; Mk. 3:31-35, Lk. 8:19-21) when discussing Christ's *weltauunschaung*, or Jesus' problems with his family (Matt. 13:53-58; Mk. 6:1-6). The New Testament genealogies of Christ are of little help since they do not mention women (cf. Matt. 1:1-17; cp. Lk. 3:23-38). The foundation for the theory that Christ was an only child can be supported with the references Jesus made dismantling the family bonds and ties (Matt. 19:27-29; Mk. 10:28-30; Lk. 12:51-53, and 14:26-27; John is silent).

[3] Cp. Lk. 13:12; cp. Matt. 24:39-41, with a parallel in Lk. 17: 34-36; cf. Jn 6:35. See also, *Mary in the New Testament*, Raymond Brown, *et al.* (Philadelphia: Fortress, 1978), pp. 157-162; Ephiphanius of Salamis, *Adversus Haer*. XLII:11.6, 70; GCS XXXI:31, 116, 13-14-42, 11, 15, 70, p. 152, 1-2.

[4] Cf. H. Räisänen, *Die Mutter Jesu im Neuen Testament* (Helsinki, 1969), p. 138f.

[5] G. G. Blum, "Das Amt der Frau im Neuen Testament," in *Novum Testamentum* VII (1964), pp. 143-44.

[6] See my *Woman as Priest, Bishop and Laity in the Early Catholic Church to 440 A.D.* (Mesquite, 1983) *passim*.

[7] Vol. I, *Gospel of Peter*, pp. 186-187; *Epistula Apostolorum*, pp. 195-96; *Gospel of Mani*, pp. 353-354.

[8] J.-P. Migne, *Patrologia. . .Latina*, vol. 112, col. 1474B; the acerbic doctor, Bernard of Clairvaux, is in Migne, *Patrologia...Latina*, vol. 183, col. 1148. Cf. Elisabeth Schussler Fiorenza, "Women Apostles: the Testament of Scripture," in *Women and Catholic Priesthood: An Expanded Vision, Proceedings of the Detroit Ordination Conference*, ed. Anne Marie Gardiner (New York, 1975), pp. 94-102; cp. *Declaration on the Question of the Admission of Women to the Ministerial Priesthood, from the Sacred Congregation for the Doctrine of the Faith* (Rome, 1977).

Chapter Two
Women in the Teachings of Jesus

Jesus taught in parables, or stories with a message (Lk. 8:10). For each story that has a masculine image there is another story that is feminine in imagery, defining more sharply Christ's own androgynous approach to humankind. In every case there is no superior sex. When the two sexes come together in a common story, man is not elevated above woman, nor is woman more powerful than man, for Christ believed that God was not a respector of persons.

In many of the parables by Jesus, woman is presented in a fashion showing her to be in a struggle with the male dominated society which is determined to continue her suppression. Frequently the woman Jesus selected was a widow—traditionally a defenseless position for any woman to be in, inasmuch as she could not inherit property (Num. 27:1-11—unless there was no son born to her father, but even in that case it was expected of her to remarry quickly and keep the property within the clan: Num. 36:1-9):

Then he told them a parable about the need to pray continually and never lose heart. "There was a judge in a certain town," he said, "who had neither fear of God nor respect for humans. In the same town there was a widow who kept on coming to him and saying, 'I want justice from you against my enemy!' For a long time he refused, but at last he said to himself, 'Maybe I have neither fear of God nor respect for humans, but since she keeps pestering me I must give this widow her just rights, or she will persist in coming and worrying

Ἔλεγε δὲ παραβολὴν αὐτοῖς πρὸς το δεῖν πάντοτε προσεύχεσθαιαὐτοὺς καὶ μὴ ἐγκακεῖν λέγων Κριτής τις ἦν ἔν τωι πόλει τὸν Θεὸν μὴ φοβούμενος καὶ ἄνθρωπον μν ἐντρεπόμενος· χήρε δὲ ἦν ἐν τῆ πόλει ἐκείμη καὶ ἤρχετο πρὸς αὐτὸν λέγουσα Ἐκδίκησόν με ἀπὸ τοῦ ἀντιδίκου μου· καὶ οὐκ ἤθελεν ἐπὶ χρόνον· μετὰ δὲ ταῦτα εἶπεν ἐν ἑαυτῶ Εἰ καὶ τὸν Θεὸν οὐ φοβοῦμαι οὐδὲ ἄνθρωπον ἐντρέπομαι διά γε τὸ παρέχειν μοι κόπον τὴν χήραν εκδικησω αὐτήν ἵνα μὴ εἰς τέλος ἐρχομένη ὑπωπιάζη με· εἶπε δὲ ὁ Κύριος Ἀκούσατε τί ὁ κριτὴς

me to death.' "

And the Lord said, "You notice what the unjust judge has to say? Now will not God see justice done to his chosen who cry out to him day and night even when he delays to help them? I promise you he will see justice done to them, and done speedily."

τῆς ἀδικίας λέγει· ὁ δὲ Θεὸς
οὐ μὴ ποιήσῃ τὴν ἐκδίκησιν τῶν
ἐκλεκτῶν αὐτοῦ τῶν βοώντων
αὐτῷ ἡμέρας καὶ νυκτός καὶ
μακροθυμεῖ ἐπ αὐτοῖς λέγω ὑμῖν
ὅτι ποιήσει τὴν ἐκδίκησιν αὐτῶν
ἐν τάχει· πλὴν ὁ υἱὸς τοῦ
ἀνθρώπου ἐλθὼν ἆρα εὑρήσει
τὴν πίστιν ἐπὶ τῆς γῆς

(Lk. 18:1-8)

The same concern with a woman's plight and poverty is pictured in the parable of the woman with ten drachmas who, if she loses one drachma, will "light a lamp and sweep the entire house and search thoroughly till she finds it; and, then when it is found, calls together her friends and neighbors, at which time she would exclaim "Rejoice with me, for I have found the drachma which I had lost" (Lk. 15:8-10), paralleling it with his concept of how God will seek out one sinner to save among the ten who would already be saved.

Or, again, what woman with ten drachmas would not, if she lost one, light a lamp and sweep out the house and search thoroughly till she found it? And then, when she had found it, call together her friends and neighbours? 'Rejoice with me,' she would say, 'I have found the drachma I lost.' In the same way, I tell you, there is rejoicing among the angels of God over one repentant sinner.

Ἢ τίς γινὴ δραχμὰς ἔχουσα
δέκα ἐὰν ἀπολέσῃ δραχμὴν
μίαν οὐχὶ ἅπτει λύχνον καὶ σαροῖ
τὴν οἰκίαν καὶ ζητεῖ ἐπιμελῶς
ἕως ὅτου εὑρῃ; καὶ εὑροῦσα
συγκαλεῖ τὰς φίλας καὶ γείτονας
λέγουσα Συγχάρητέ μοι ὅτι
εὗρον τὴν δραχμὴν ἣν ἀπώλεσα·
οὕτω λέγω ὑμῖν γίνεται χαρὰ
ἐνώπιον τῶν ἀγγέλων τοῦ Θεοῦ
ἐπί ἑνὶ ἁμερτωλῷ μετανοοῦντι·

Jesus' concern for impoverished widows is highlighted in his comment concerning the presentation of a life's savings to the treasury by one woman destitute save for two small coins worth approximately one penny:

He sat down opposite the treasury and watched the people putting money into the treasury, and many of the rich put in a great deal. A poor widow came and put in two small coins, the equivalent of one penny. Then he called his disciples and said to them, "I tell you solemnly, this poor widow has put in more than all who have contributed to the treasury; for they have all put in money they had [left] over [above their needs], but she—from the little she had—has put in everything she possessed, all she had to live on."

Καὶ καθίσας κατέναντι τοῦ γαζοφυλακίου ἐθεώρει πῶς ὁ ὄχλος βάλλει χαλκὸν εἰς τὸ γαζοφυλάκιον καὶ πολλοὶ πλούσιοι ἔβαλλον πολλά· καὶ ἐλθοῦσα μία χήρα πτωχὴ ἔβαλε λεπτὰ δύο ὅ ἐστι κοδράντης· καὶ προσκαλεσάμενος τοὺς μαθητὰς αὐτοῦ εἶπεν αὐτοῖς Ἀμὴν λέγω ὑμῖν ὅτι ἡ χήρα αὕτη ἡ πτωχὴ πλεῖον πάντων ἔβαλε τῶν βαλλόντων εἰς τὸ γαζοφυλάκιον πάντες γὰρ ἐκ τοῦ περισσεύοντος αὐτοῖς ἔβαλον αὐτὴ δὲ ἐκ τῆς ὑστερήσεως αὐτῆς πάντα ὅσα εἶχεν ἔβαλεν ὅλον τὸν βίον αὐτῆς

(Mk. 12:41-44; cp. Lk. 21:1-4)

The abuse and impoverishment of widows Jesus condemned soundly (Lk. 20:45-47):

While all the people were listening, he said to the disciples, "Beware of the scribes who like to walk about in long robes and love to be greeted obsequiously in the market squares, to take the front seats in the synagogues and the places of honor at banquets, who swallow the property of widows, while making a show of lengthy prayers. The more severe will be the sentence they receive.

Ἀκούοντος δὲ παντὸς τοῦ λαοῦ εἶπε τοῖς μαθηταῖς αὐτοῦ Προσέχετε ἀπὸ τῶν γραμματέων τῶν θελόντων περιπατεῖν ἐν στολαῖς καὶ φιλούντων ἀσπασμοὺς ἐν ταῖς ἀγοραῖς καὶ πρωτοκαθεδρίας ἐν ταῖς συναγωγαῖς καὶ πρωτοκλισίας ἐν τοῖς δείπνοις οἱ κατεσθίουσι τὰς οἰκίας τῶν χηρῶν καὶ προφάσει μακρὰ προσεύχονται οὗτοι λήψονται περισσότερον κρίμα·

Christ's compassion for the widow was so strong that he quickly performed miracles to aid them, as he did with the widow of Nain (Lk. 7:11-17). Such actions spread his fame quickly "throughout Judea and the surrounding country."

Widows accepted prophets more quickly than others
(Lk. 24:25-27), and served as willing prophets themselves
(Lk. 2:36-38), for widows were strong in their persever-
ance in prayer and commitment (Lk. 18:1-8), whereas men
were given to more base needs and pleasures, quick to find
excuses, and unwilling to risk all that they had to firm a
commitment (Lk. 11:5-9). Thus the compassion for
women was great with Jesus, who used the weaknesses that
some women experienced as additional teaching tools. In
part Jesus' acceptance of the "sins" of some women was
because he realized that all humankind was subject to
forgetting higher values and principles. Thus he had little
difficulty in accepting being around adulteresses, "unclean"
(menstruating) women, lepers, women "possessed", or
other "untouchables" within his society. His attitude was
founded on common sense—all humankind errs, and thus
to err is human; to elevate oneself above the baseness of
humanity requires the ability to overlook and forgive; thus
Christ taught "Let him who is without sin cast the first
stone". At the same time, while Jesus was able to forgive
the adulteress, he admonished her "to go and sin no
more." This admonishment was a statement that she, too,
was to elevate herself to a greater plain of self-actualization
above that which was base. Adultery is an act of selfishness, for it hurts another. Jesus condemned this hurt, for
it was not only psychologically harmful, but denied
charity. He could not condemn the act, but only instruct
the woman to follow a different course for her life, for
ultimate judgement remained in the hands of God (Matt.
7:1).[1]

Christ's urgency to assist women is permeated
throughout the records that remain. Among these is the
unique account of the "woman bent double." Why she
was in that physical condition we can only speculate concerning; there is no definite statement in any of the
Gospels. Christ does not condemn the woman—nor does
he adjudge her affliction to be the result of some current
or past sin, nor the result of a sin committed by one of her
forefathers. Instead he says nothing, but releases the
woman from her infirmity.

Although the healing of the woman was considered miraculous, what was truly miraculous was the fact that Jesus cured the woman on the Sabbath! Not only did Jesus defend his actions, declaring "Hypòcrites! Is there one of you who does not untie his ox or his ass from the manger on the sabbath and take it out for watering?" and then with great emphasis "And this woman, a *daughter* of Abraham whom Satan has bound these eighteen years—was it not right to untie her bonds on the sabbath day?" (Lk. 13:10-17). This last statement gave the woman bent double an unparalleled equality with the men around her who prided themselves on being the "sons of Abraham."[2] She was the first to be recognized for what she was—a chosen person of God, which was to be a claim all women could make from then on (Gal. 3:7; cp. Matt. 3:8; Lk. 3:8; Jn. 8:39).

Christ's hatred of discrimination in any form found further fodder fueling heated controversy with the establishment, the society in which he lived and moved. Not only did he blast those who forbade work on the sabbath when such work was necessary for the health, safety and sanity of an individual, but he rejected the lines that he had to be associated with socially acceptable people. Neither a xenophobe nor a isolate, Jesus conversed with all people: the antecedent for his later command to his apostles to "go forth, to all nations". This message was dramatically emphasized when he met and conversed with the woman of Samaria at the well (Jn. 4:1-42). Openly he was untroubled and unconcerned with the prominent public opinion that he was talking to an "outcast". As far as he was concerned, there were no outcasts in heaven (Jn. 4:27) and thus he would recognize no taboos either. Additionally, during his conversation with the woman of Samaria, Jesus was able to test her faith—and found it stronger than the faith of most of those "chosen" people who lived and moved around him (Jn. 4:28, 39). In fact, according to the records we possess, her faith was so strong that she became his first missionary—long before any of his male apostles went abroad to preach the name and teach the faith of the man from Galilee. Through the power of Christ she became the first *evangelion* (evangelist) for "Many Samaritans of that town had believed on the strength of the *woman's* testimony. . . ." (*episteusan dia ton logon*; cp. Jn. 17:20: *pisteuonton dia tou logou*, Christ's prayer at the Last Supper). So powerful was the persuasive ability of the woman that Jesus stayed an extra two days in her town, and spoke to "the many" who came to see and hear him, so that, after hearing Christ "they said to the *woman*, "Now we . . . know that he really is the saviour of the world." (Jn. 4:42).

Women not only were the first evangelists in the movement established by Christ, but were also the first to anoint him, and then call him "The Anointed One"—or Christ (Christus). Mary performed the first act of anointing him, which brought about immediate scandal, for this Mary was undoubtedly a town prostitute (*en hamartolos*), since she had loose hair. Loose hair was grounds for mandatory divorce, since a woman was never to let her hair be uncovered in public, as only prostitutes let their hair fall loosely about their shoulders. She sought Christ out to repent of her sins, and in gratitude for his forgiveness bathed his feet with her tears and dried them with her hair. "Then she covered his feet with kisses and anointed them with the ointment" which she had brought in an alabaster jar (Lk. 7:36-50).

Later, Mary of Bethany anointed Christ's head with an ointment so costly that it was considered a treasure fit only for kings (Matt. 26:6-13; Mk. 14:3-9; Jn. 12:1-8). And, finally, his body would be anointed a third time before Christ would be entombed, surrendering his soul upon the cross.

Synthesizing these three accounts, we can see many parallels with Christ's life, passion and death. Hypothesizing on quite firm grounds, we can conclude that Christ's life and actions were as much a teaching device as his lectures (or sermons) and parables. Whereas he quarreled with various men in his day, there is no record of any heated exchange between himself and a woman, nor is there any account of his condemning women (or any woman in particular) as he did the Pharisees and other male Jews. In fact, Jesus damned the pretensiousness and psuedo-religiosity of the chief priests and elders, rebuking them with the scornful appellation of "Hypocrites!" and declaring, soundly

"I tell you solemnly, tax collectors and prostitutes are making their way into the reign of God before you. For John came to you, a pattern of true righteousness, but you did not believe him, and yet the tax collectors and prostitutes did."

... Ἰησοῦς Ἀμὴν λέγω ὑμῖν ὅτι οἱ τελῶναι καὶ αἱ πόρναι προάγουσιν ὑμᾶς εἰς τὴν βασιλείαν τοῦ Θεοῦ· ἦλθε γὰρ πρὸς ὑμᾶς Ἰωάννης ἐν ὁδῷ δικαιοσύνης καὶ οὐκ ἐπιστεύσατε αὐτῷ· οἱ δὲ τελῶναι καὶ αἱ πόρναι ἐπίστευσαν αὐτῷ· ὑμεῖς δὲ ἰδόντες οὐδὲ μετεμελήθητε ὕστερον τοῦ πιστεῦσαι αὐτῷ·

(Matt. 21:31-32).

The word "prostitute" is used only once by Jesus. Usually the Synoptic Gospels use the term "tax collectors and sinners"—strong evidence that the word, in this case, came directly from Jesus. He did not damn prostitutes—as did his society; instead he declared that prostitutes would be saved before the hypocrites who feign religion. This was because he was opposed to any person being reduced only to a sex object, as was the destiny and lot of women who earned their living only by selling their bodies for sex. Therefore, Jesus saw prostitutes as objects of exploitation, and not an object to be disdained. He felt pity and compassion and loved them when no one else would love them. It is true that the lot of the prostitute (*pornai*) may have been that of the "sinful woman" of Lk. 7:38-50, and that of the adulterous woman in Jn. 8:2-11, but the word is not used. Even then, however, Jesus shows compassion—a compassion similar in nature and extent, for in each case the woman was abused by men, taken advantage of by men, and disregarded and shunned by men, as if their livelihood was a sign of their personal, psychological debasedness, and a clue of intellectual ignorance.

Women were not (and are not!) ignorant. Nor did Jesus see women as intellectual misfits, nor ignoramuses. Instead the Gospels show that women were educated, and knew their history, religious destiny, and were able to recognize that which other scholars (read, rabbis, scribes, and Pharisees) overlooked (Lk. 11:27-28). Women also had common sense which enabled women to surmount difficulties and losses (Mk. 4:2-4, 21-22; cf. Lk. 8:4-8, 16-17). To that end, he used female images in his parables and teachings: comparing heaven to the leaven in dough which "a *woman* took and mixed in with three measures of flour till it was leavened throughout" (Lk. 13:20-21; cf. Matt. 13:33), placed lamps on lampstands so what was lost could be found (Lk. 8:4-8; cf. Matt. 13:4-9; Mk. 4:1-9); swept the house until all which was lost was found (Lk. 15:1-5); lead armies against the degenerate who would not recognize God (Matt. 12:38-42; cf. Lk. 11:29-32); keep oil in their lamps (Matt. 25:1-13), all which were in comparison with the Godhead which Jesus gave feminine attributes to—as he gave himself, as when he lamented, "Jerusalem, Jerusalem, you that kill the prophets and stone those who are sent to you! How often have I longed to gather your children, as a hen gathers her brood under her wings, and you refuse!" (Lk. 13:34; cf. Matt. 23:37). Or, more graphically:

On the last and greatest day of the festival, Jesus stood there and cried out: "If anyone is thirsty, let him come to me! Let him come and drink who believes in me! As scripture says, 'From his breast (*koilia*) shall flow fountains of living water.' " He was speaking of the Spirit which those who believed in him were to receive; for there was no Spirit as yet because Jesus had not yet been glorified.

Ἐν δὲ τῇ ἐσχάτῃ ἡμέρᾳ τῇ μεγάλῃ τῆς ἑορτῆ εἱστήκει ὁ Ἰησοῦς καὶ ἔκραξε λέγων Ἐάν τις διψᾷ ἐρχέσθω πρός με καὶ πινέτω· ὁ πιστεύων εἰς ἐμέ καθὼς εἶπεν ἡ γραφή ποταμοὶ ἐκ τῆς κοιλίας αὐτοῦ ῥεύσουσιν ὕδατος ζῶντος· τοῦτο δὲ εἶπε περὶ τοῦ Πνεύματος οὗ ἔμελλον λαμβάνιεν οἱ πιστεύσαντες εἰς αὐτον· οὔπω γὰρ ἦν Πνεῦμα ὅτι ὁ Ἰησοῦς οὔπω ἐδοξάσθη

(Jn. 7:37-39).

This rapport, led Jesus into recognizing the unique ministry of women. Not only had women ministered to him (Lk. 8:1-3), but Jesus charged women to minister to the needs of the world.

NOTES

[1] See my *Woman, Sex & Religion* (Mesquite, 1984). Cf. Bruce M. Metzger, *A Textual Commentary on the Greek New Testament* (United Bible Societies, 1971), pp. 219ff. The passage in the Gospel of John is of dubious authenticity and historicity, for it (Jn. 7:53-8:11) is absent from the two oldest copies of the Gospel: the Bodmer Codex (Papyrus 66; written sometime in the third century, and Papyrus 75, which can be dated somewhere between 175 A.D. and 225 A.D. as to time of authorship). At the same time, this key passage is missing from other ancient Greek manuscripts—many of which were written on vellum. It is not incorporated into any printed version until 1516, appearing only in Tyndale's 1525 English edition. Prior to its incorporation in 1525, it had been appended and/or asterisked—showing it to be of problematic origin. See my *Woman and the Gospel of John* (Los Angeles: Woman's Awareness Press, 1973), pp. 231f.

[2] Male Jews were called *bnei brith* ("sons of the covenant").

Chapter Three
Women in the Ministry of Jesus

The fullness of the responsibility of women in the ministry for Jesus is contained in the eighth chapter of Luke. The first sentence, which is quite long in the Greek, confirms the importance of women, for women are included in the number of those who accompanied Jesus through the cities and towns he travelled, preaching and teaching, winning souls, and healing by faith unbridled:

Now after this he made his way through towns and villages preaching and proclaiming the Good News of the reign of God; with him went the Twelve [male apostles] as well as certain women who had been cured of evil spirits and ailments: Mary, surnamed the Magdalene, from whom seven demons had gone out; Joanna, the wife of Herod's steward Chuza; Suzanna, and several others who ministered (*diekonoun*) to them out of their own resources.

Καὶ ἐγένετο ἐν τῶ καθεξῆς καὶ αὐτὸς διώδενε κατὰ πόλιν καὶ κώμην κηρύσσων καὶ εὐαγγελιζόμενος τὴν βασιλείαο τοῦ Θεοῦ καὶ οἱ δώδεκα σὺν αὐτῶ καὶ γυναῖκές τινες αἳ ἦσαν τεθεραπευμένα ἀπὸ πνευμάτων πονηρῶν καὶ ἀσθενειῶν Μαρία ἡ καλουμένη Μαγδαληνή ἀφ' ἧς δαιμόνια ἑπτὰ ἐξεληλύθει καὶ Ἰωάννα γυνὴ Χουζᾶ ἐπιτρόπου Ἡρώδου καὶ Σουσάννα καὶ ἕτεραι πολλαί αἵτινες διηκόνουν αὐτοις ἐκ τῶν ὑπαρχόντων αὐταῖς

Luke ascribes to the women their ministerial tasks (*diakonos*), which is identical to the duties assigned to the men who followed Jesus (cf. Lk. 7:36-50). All three of the Synoptic Gospels use the verb *diakoneo* (to minister, or, to serve) to describe the duties of these women—*in addition* to saying that they "followed" Jesus.

There were some women watching from a distance. Among them were Mary of Magdala, Mary who was the mother of James the younger and Joset,

ἦσαν δὲ καὶ γυναῖκες ἀπὸ μακρόθεν θεωροῦσαι ἐν αἷς καὶ Μαρία ἡ Μαγδαληνή καὶ Μαρία ἡ τοῦ Ἰακώβου τοῦ μικροῦ καὶ Ἰωσῆ μήτηρ, καὶ Σαλώμη αἵ

and Salome. These used to
follow him and minister
(*diekonoun*) to him when he was
in Galilee. And there were many
other *women* there who had
come up to Jerusalem with him.

ὅτε ἦν ἐν τῇ Γαλιλαία
ἠκολούθουν αὐτῶ καὶ
διηκόνουν αὐτω καὶ ἄλλαι
πολλαὶ αἱ συναναβᾶσαι αὐτῷ
εἰς Ἱεροσόλυμα

(Mk. 15:40-41)

And many women were there,
watching from a distance, the
same women who had followed
Jesus from Galilee and ministered (*diakonousai*) to him. Among
them were Mary of Magdala,
Mary the mother of James and
Joseph, and the mother of
Zebedee's sons.

ἦσαν δὲ ἐκεῖ γυναῖκες πολλαὶ
ἀπὸ μακρόθεν θεωροῦσαι αἵτινες
ἠκολούθησαν τῷ Ἰησοῦ ἀπὸ τῆς
Γαλιλαίας διακονοῦσαι αὐτῷ· ἐν
αἷς ἦν Μαρία ἡ Μαγδαληνή καὶ
Μαρία ἡ τοῦ Ἰακώβου καὶ
Ἰωσῆ μήτηρ καὶ ἡ μήτηρ τῶν
υἱῶν Ζεβεδαίου

(Matt. 27:55-56).

The early Church recognized these women as disciples
(*matheteuein*), as it did the twelve men (*mathetes*) who
followed Christ.[1] Jesus certainly encouraged these women
to study—a vocation and discipline that was anathema to
the orthodox Jewish male who believed that formal learning, such as the skills of reading and writing, belonged only
to men. This can be seen quite easily in the account of
the evening Jesus spent with Mary and Martha, for Mary
took for herself the traditional male role and "sat at the
feet of Jesus and listened to his teaching"—a stock phrase
used by orthodox rabbis to indicate a person studying the
words of a rabbi (teacher). Martha's undoubtedly thought
that Mary was breaking tradition and accepted custom—
that Mary was in error for choosing the role of a student
and scholar. Jesus did not agree with her and so rebuked
her, declaring that Mary had chosen the best way to
occupy her time, that women were called to the intellectual life as were men, and thus also merit salvation:

In the course of their journey he

Ἐν δὲ τῷ πορεύεσθαι αὐτοὺς

came to a village, and a woman named Martha welcomed him into her house. She had a sister called Mary, who sat down at the feet of the Lord and listened to him speaking. Now Martha who was distracted with all the serving said, "Lord, do you not care that my sister is leaving me to do all the serving by myself? Please tell her to help me." But the Lord answered: "Martha, Martha," he said, "you worry and fret about so many things, and yet few are needed, indeed only one. It is Mary who has chosen the better part; it is not to be taken from her.

αὐτὸς εἰσῆλθεν εἰς κώμην τινά·
γυνὴ δέ τις ὀνόματι Μάρθα
ὑπεδέξατο αὐτὸν εἰς τὸν οἶκον
αὐτῆς· καὶ τῆδε ἦν ἀδελφὴ
καλουμένη Μαρία ἣ καὶ
παρακαθεσθεῖσα πρὸς τοὺς
πόδας τοῦ Κυρίου ἤκουε τὸν
λόγον αὐτοῦ· ἡ δὲ Μάρθα
περιεσπᾶτο περὶ πολλὴν
διακονίαν· ἐπιστᾶσα δὲ εἶπε
Κύριε οὐ μέλει σοι ἡ ἀδελ-
φή μου μόνην με κατέλειπε
διακονέω εἰπε οὖν αὐτῃ ἵνα μοι
συναντιλάβηται, ἀποκριθεὶς δὲ
εἶπεν αὐτῇ ὁ Κύριος Μάρθα
Μάρθα μεριμνᾶς καὶ θορυβάζῃ
περὶ πολλά· ἑνὸς δέ ἐστι χρεία·
Μαρία γὰρ τὴν ἀγαθὴν μερίδα
ἐξελέξατο ἥτις οὐκ
ἀφαιρεθήσεται ἀπ' αὐτῆς.

(Lk. 10:38-42).

Another incident which confirms Jesus' attitude toward the intellectual life of women appears a little later in Luke's account. Jesus is preaching. A woman from the crowd raises her voice to pay him a compliment. She applauded his mother—reducing the mother of Jesus to a sexual entity, acclaiming her for her generational prowess—or, if you wish to use current terminology, being a "baby machine". Jesus abruptly rejects her contention and belief that the purpose of women is to only bear children. Instead, he insists that a woman is a *person* in the eyes of God, whose intellectual faculties are of greater value and importance than is her sexual reproductive abilities.

Now, as he was speaking, a woman in the crowd raised her voice and said, "Happy the womb that bore you and the

Ἐγένετο δὲ ἐν τῷ λέγειν αὐτὸν
ταῦτα ἐπάρασά τις φωνὴν γυνὴ
ἐκ του ὄχλου εἶπεν αὐτῷ
Μακαρία η κοιλία ἡ βαστάσασά

breasts you sucked!" But he replied, "Blessed rather are those who hear the word of God and keep it!"

σε καὶ μαστοὶ οὓς ἐθήλασας· αὐτὸς δὲ εἶπε Μενοῦν μακάριοι οἱ ἀκούοντες τὸν λόγον τοῦ Θεοῦ καὶ φυλάσσοντες

(Lk. 11:27-28).

This statement is quite in keeping with the general character of Jesus. Repeatedly he rejected the traditional restrictive family ties of his society, claiming that the only true family he and/or God could recognize is the family of humankind which would come to him and/or to God in quest of knowledge and thereby earn mental and spiritual salvation which is equated with immortality—or "eternal life."

And everyone who has left houses, brothers, sisters, father, mother, children or land for the sake of my name will be repaid a hundred times over, and also inherit eternal life.

καὶ πᾶς ὃς ἀφῆκεν οἰκίας ἢ ἀδελφοὺς ἢ ἀδελφὰς ἢ πατέρα ἢ μητέρα ἢ τέκνα ἢ ἀγρούς ἕνεκεν τοῦ ὀνόματός μου ἑκατονταπλασίονα λήψεται καὶ ζωὴν αἰώοιθο κληρονομήσει-

(Matt. 19:29); and

Peter took this up, "What about us?" he asked him. "We have left everything and followed you." Jesus said, "I tell you solemnly, there is no one who has left house, brothers, sisters, father, children, or land for my sake and for the sake of the gospel who will not be repaid a hundred times over, houses, brothers, sisters, mothers, children and land—not without persecutions—now in this present time, and in the world to come eternal life.

ἤρξατο ὁ Πέτρος λέγειν αὐτῶ Ἰδοὺ ἡμεῖς ἀφήκαμεν πάντα καὶ ἠκολουθήκαμεν σοι ἔφη ὁ Ιησοῦς Ἀμὴν λέγω ὑμῖν οὐδείς εστιν ὃς ἀφῆκεν οἰκίαν ἢ ἀδελφοὺς ἢ ἀδελφὰς ἢ μητερα η πατερα ἢ τεκνα ἢ ἀγροὺς ἕνεκεν ἐμου καὶ ἕνεκεν τοῦ εὐαγγελίου ἐὰν μὴ λάβῃ ἑκατονταπλασίονα νῦν ἐν τῶ καιρῶ τούτω οἰκίας καὶ ἀδελφοὺς καὶ ἀδελφὰς καὶ μητέρας καὶ τέκνα και ἀγροὺς μετά διωγμῶν καὶ εν τῶ αἰῶνι τῶ ἐρχομένω ζωὴν αἰώνιον·

(Mk. 10:28-30).

He demanded exclusive love. "Anyone who prefers father or mother to me is not worthy of me. Anyone who prefers a son or daughter to me is not worthy of me."

(Matt. 10:37-38). Jesus was a realist. He knew that it would not be easy for anyone to love him—for by loving him there would be problems, social questioning and ridicule, injury, and even the possibility of death (Matt. 10:34-36). Whereas men would be more cautious inasmuch as they had more to lose socially, personally, and financially, women, who were already socially and economically disinherited and disenfranchised, had little if anything to lose. Therefore, women could join his coterie and accept an apostleship more quickly and easily than could men— especially if they were "public sinners" and other outcasts, or women in societies which were outcast as a group. Thus the Samaritans "believed. . .because of the woman's word (*episteusan dia ton logon*)" (Jn. 4:38-42).[2]

Much of the actual discipleship of and by women occurred after the physical death of Jesus. This was unique. Jesus' male disciples deserted him: "Then all the [male] disciples deserted him and ran away" (Matt. 26: 56). Even at his crucifixion "those who knew" Jesus stood at a distance and watched—although in the Gospel of John it does say that "the disciple Jesus loved," was below the cross, (Jn. 19:25-27) but contemporary scholarship discounts this passage as being a later addition. We must follow current historical scholarship and turn to the accounts in Matthew, Mark and Luke (although there is debate on the historical authenticity of the passage also in Luke, believing it to contain unhistorical additions to the reports left by both Matthew and Mark) which declare that only women were with Jesus in his final hours (Matt. 27:55-56; Mk. 15:40-41; Lk. 23: 49). Women remained with Jesus at the moment of his death. Women petitioned Nicodemus and Joseph of Arimathaea to obtain the body of Jesus for burial. With these two members of the Council, women alone buried Jesus. "Mary of Magdala and Mary the mother of Joset were watching and took note of where he was laid" (Mk. 15:47), for "Mary of Magdala and the other Mary were there, sitting opposite the sepulchre." (Matt. 27:61). After the body was placed in the tomb, women "returned and prepared spices and ointments." for his entombment (Matt. 27:57-61; Mk. 15:42-47; Lk. 23: 50-56). Women, again, were the first persons to have the opportunity to witness the empty tomb; women were the first to hear the message that Jesus had been resurrected from the dead—which was initially rejected by the male disciples who stayed enchained to the Jewish custom of forbidding women to witness and carry testimony to men (Matt. 28:1-8)

After the sabbath, and towards dawn of the first day of the week, Mary of Magdala and the other Mary went to visit the sepulchre. And all at once there was a violent earthquake, for the angel of the Lord, descending from heaven, came and rolled away the stone and sat on it. His face was like lightning and his robe was white as snow. The guards were so shaken, so frightened of him, that they were like dead men. But the angel spoke, and he said to the *women*, "There is no need for you to be afraid. I know you are looking for Jesus, who was crucified; he is not here, for he has risen, as he said he would. Come, and see the place where he lay, then go quickly and tell his disciples, 'He has risen from the dead and now he is going before you to Galilee—it is there you will see him.' Now I have told you." Filled with awe and great joy the women came quickly away from the tomb and ran to tell the disciples.

Ὀψὲ δὲ σαββάτων τῇ ἐπιφωσκούσῃ εἰς μίαν σαββάτων ἦλθε Μαρία ἡ Μαγδαληνή καὶ ἡ ἄλλη Μαρία θεωρῆσαι τὸν τάφον καὶ ἰδού σειεμὸς ἐγένετο μέγας· ἄγγελος γὰρ Κυρίου καταβὰς ἐξ οὐρανοῦ καὶ προσελθὼν ἀπεκύλισε τὸν λίθον καὶ ἐκάθητο ἐπάνω αὐτοῦ ἦν δὲ ἡ ἰδέα αὐτου ὡς ἀστραπή καὶ τὸ ἔνδυμα αὐτοῦ λευκὸν ὡσεὶ χιών. ἀπὸ δὲ τοῦ φόβου αὐτου ἐσείσθησαν οἱ τηροῦντες καὶ ἐγένοντο ὡστεὶ νεκροί ἀποκριθεὶς δὲ ὁ ἄγγελος εἶπε ταῖς γυναιξί Μὴ φοβεῖσθε υμεῖς οἶδα γὰρ ὅτι Ἰησοῦν τὸν ἐσταυρωμένον ζητεῖτε οὐκ ἔστιν ὧδε° ἠγέρθη γὰρ κεθὼς εἶπε δεῦτε ἴδετε τὸν τόπον ὅπου ἔκειτο ὁ Κύριος. καὶ ταχὺ πορευθεῖσαι εἴτατε τοῖς μαθηταῖς αὐτοῦ ὅτι Ἠγέρθη ἀπὸ τῶν νεκρῶν° καὶ ἰδού προάγει ὑμᾶς εἰς τὴν Γαλιλαίαν· ἐκεῖ αὐτόν ὄψεσθε ἰδού εἶπον ὑμῖν καὶ ἀπελθοῦσαι ταχὺ ἀπὸ τοῦ μνημείου μετὰ φόβου καὶ χαρᾶς μεγάλης ἔδραμον ἀπεγγεῖλαι τοῖς μαθηταῖς αὐτοῦ.

The account in Mark (16:1-8) is even more emphatic that the male disciples were not there, for the angel declared:

'...You are looking for Jesus of Nazareth, who was crucified: he has risen, he is not here. See, here is the place where they laid him. But you must go and tell his disciples and Peter, 'He is going before you to Galilee, it is there you will see him, just as he told you.' "And the *women* came out and ran away from the tomb because they were frightened out of their wits; and they said nothing to anyone [at that time] for they were afraid."

...Ἰησοῦν ζητεῖτε τὸν Ναζαρηνὸν τὸν ἐσταυρωμένον· ἠγέρθη οὐκ ἔστιν ὦδε· ἴδε ὁ τόπος ὅπου ἔθηκαν αὐτόν ἀλλ᾽ ὑπάγετε εἴπατε τοῖς μαθηταῖς αὐτοῦ καὶ τῳ Πέτρῳ ὅτι Προάγει ὑμᾶς εἰς τὴν Γαλιλαίαν· ἐκεῖ αὐτὸν ὄψεσθε καθὼς εἶπεν ὑμῖν καὶ ἐξελθοῦσαι ἔφυγον ἀπὸ τοῦ μνημείου εἶχε γὰρ αὐτὰς τρόμος καὶ ἔκστασις· καὶ οὐδενὶ οὐδὲν εἶπον ἐφοβοῦντο γάρ

That the women's fright was only temporary is confirmed in the account of Matthew (cf. 1. 8): "Filled with awe and great joy the women came quickly away from the tomb and ran to tell the disciples." The fact that the women went to witness to the male disciples of the resurrection of Christ is in a very real sense a statement that they, too, were *apostoloi* (apostles).

The full number of women apostles who witnessed the resurrection of Jesus to the world can not be confirmed. The accounts vary. Matthew says "Mary of Magdala and the other Mary went to visit the sepulchre." (Matt. 28:1). Mark states that "Mary of Magdala, Mary, the mother of James, and Salome brought spices with which to go and anoint him" (Mk. 16:1). Luke declares that "the women were Mary of Magdala, Joanna, and Mary the mother of James" and then adds *the other women with them also told the apostles* (Lk. 24:10-11). John the Evangelist, who wrote considerably later than the other Gospel writers and thus could have had a more failed memory, states that only one woman–Mary of Magdala–visited the tomb and then witnessed the resurrection to the apostles (Jn. 20:1). All of the writers, however, agree, that none of the men believed the women at first; but Peter, who went "running to the tomb" was "amazed" when he "saw the binding cloths but nothing else." (Lk. 24:12). John gives us the greatest mystery, for he interjects "then the other disciple who had reached the tomb first also went in [after Peter] ;

and he saw and he believed". Who is the other disciple? A male is all we can know for certain—but it undoubtedly was John himself, since the term "the other disciple" is presented to the reader twice before this critical line. Then, too, one needs to consider the line "Till this moment they had failed to understand the teaching of scripture, that he must rise from the dead." This can only be applicable to the two disciples: Peter, and undoubtedly John, since the women had already testified as to the resurrection of Jesus, and had no recorded doubts.

The last part of this discovery, "the disciples then went home again" could refer either to the male disciples, or the female apostles, or both. There is no way of determining, but it would make the greatest sense to interpret it to mean both the men and the women went home since it would have been inane for the women to remain at the empty tomb.

But even here the ministry of women in the message of the Christ continues, for Jesus later appeared—again to a woman—Mary of Magdala (Mk. 16:9-11). Matthew, on the other hand, says that Christ appeared to both Mary of Magdala and "the other Mary". In his account we find the first direct commissioning of women to the apostleship of Jesus by Jesus himself—since they were "sent" (*apostellein*) to bear witness to his resurrection (Matt. 28:9-10)

And there, coming to meet them was Jesus. "Greetings," he said. And the women came up to him and, falling down before him, clasped his feet. Then Jesus said to them, "Do not be afraid: *go and tell my brothers* that they must leave for Galilee; they will see me there.	και ιδου ο Ιησους απηντησεν αυτις λεγων Χαιρετε αι δε προσελθουσαι εκρατησαν αυτου τους ποδας και προσεκυνησαν αυτω τοτε λεγει αυταις ο Ιησους Μη φοβεισθε• υπαγγειλατε τοις αδελφοις μου ινα απελθωσιν εις την Γαλιλαιαν κακει με οψβνται

In John's account (Jn. 20:11-18), Mary of Magdala, is directly addressed as "woman" *twice*, and then called by name, afterwhich she declared him to be her teacher, using the Hebrew word *Rabbuni*. Upon her affirmation of faith, Jesus commissioned her to be the first of the apostles: for she was to be an apostle to the apostles. It is on this statement by Christ that Bernard of Clairvaux was able also to award the Magdalena the appellation of being the "apostle to the apostles". Moreover, this comment by Christ is a clear and definitive statement rejecting the traditionally held theory on the "inferiority of women." Men, now, had to broaden their perspectives, reevaluate their thinking, and shed the shackles of time honored ignorance—which, unfortunately, still has not fully occurred as can be seen in traditional Christianity of the twentieth century when Pope John Paul II and the Vatican can have the unChristian, unBiblical, and uncharitable gall to decree that women were not and shall never be ordained to the priesthood of Christ—when Christ himself commissioned women to that very role. But not only is it the lack of Christian understanding within the Vatican, and especially in the person of the Vicar of Christ, that is to be lamented, but it is still strangling many other denominations within the Christian community. *Man* has not yet realized, or at least recognized, that *he* is only a part of the broad creation of humankind, and still lives in the fantasy of ignorance where *he* is somehow special and set apart and above woman. Until this changes, full and true Christianity will never be realized on earth—or elsewhere. How strange it is that what is called the Aprocyphal Writings can strengthen and compliment Scripture, whereas those Bible readers and reputed theologians cannot acknowledge it to exist as co-equal with the basic canon. The Gospel of Peter states quite clearly that Mary Magdalene was "a woman disciple of the Lord".[3]

NOTES

[1] Sophia Jesu Christi, *New Testament Apocrypha*, Vol. 1, p. 246.

[2] Raymond E. Brown, "Roles of Women in the Fourth Gospel," *Theological Studies* (December, 1975), p. 691.

[3] Gospel of Peter, *New Testament Apocyrpha*, vol. 1, pp. 186-187; cf. Migne, *Patrologia...Latina*, vol. 183, col. 1148; for the inclusion of Mary of Magdala in the Western rite canon, see Josef Andreas Jungmann, *The Mass of the Roman Rite* (Grand Rapids: Benziger Brothers, 1951), p. 470.

Chapter Four
Women in Apostolic Thought

Women were loved by Jesus. In the Gospels Jesus often used women in his stories—something quite unusual for that time and his culture which was primarily anti-woman, for Jewish society saw women as disposable, as defined in the Decalogue: "You shall not covet your neighbor's wife, nor his male, nor female slave, nor his ox or ass, nor anything else that *belongs* to him" (Ex. 20:17). Woman was property: "if a man sells his daughter as a slave, she shall not regain her liberty like male slaves" (Ex. 21:7), who he could also send out as whores (Gen. 19:4-8; Judg. 19:22-29). She was not to quarrel or refuse man's wishes, but adore him and call him *ba'al* ("master", here used as a noun: Ex. 21:4, 22; Deut. 22:22, and 24:4; II Sam. 11:26; Esther 1:17, 20, Prov. 12:4, and 31:11, 23, 28, and Joel 1:8), or *'adon* ("Lord", as in Judg. 19:26). A daughter could inherit only if there was no son to inherit (Num. 27:1-11), and was forbidden to move or marry outside of the clan for fear that the dowry would be lost (Num. 36:1-9). A woman could be punished for having sex outside of marriage, whereas a man was immune from punishment provided he did not have sex with a married or betrothed woman—an adulteress was punished for having "exposed her flesh" and for having injured her husband's property rights, while the adulterer was executed only because he had injured the husband's property rights. While men were not required to watch the stoning of an adulterer, and/or adulteress, women were required "to see it" so that they would be forewarned of their fate should they be found "guilty" of such a "crime" (Ezek. 16:37-41).[1] Jesus had none of these antediluvian and post-Exilic concerns. Instead he associated women with "the reign of heaven", and argued that women bring balance to men (Luke 8:4-8, and 16-17; cf. Mark 4:1-9,

21-22; Matt. 13:4-9, and 5:15; Luke 11:33-36; there is no gender used in the story of the lamp, instead the Greek reads *oudeis*). In Jesus' story of the widow and the unjust judge, the man is given no qualities superior to the woman (Luke 11:5-9), in fact Jesus pictures the woman as "masculine": having the masculine characteristics of aggressiveness and determination to succeed—so similar to the *eklekta kyria* of II John.

Whereas Jewish tradition had little to say about women inheriting life eternal, Matthew relates Jesus' story of the end of the world when "Of two women at the millstone grinding, one is taken, one is left" (Matt. 24:41)—quite identical to Luke's story of two women grinding at the end of time (Luke 17:36).

Jesus likened God to a woman—the woman who lost her coin and searched until it was found (Luke 15:8f.). This is picked up and embellished in the Gospel of Thomas (a third-century Gnostic Christian "extracanonical" work still debated by scholars as if its sayings can be attributable to Jesus) which states quite clearly that "the kingdom of the [Father] is like a woman" (Logion 96-97).[2]

Jesus gave woman more rights than did the rabbis. Whereas divorce was traditionally a right of men, Jesus said "and if a woman divorces her husband. . ." (Mark 10: 12), but qualified it by applying to her the same restrictions that were to be imposed on a man seeking a divorce: to separate only in cases of inchastity (*mē epi porneiai*; Matt. 19:9; Mark 5:28). Remarriage by any divorced man or woman was equally considered to be adultery; at the same time if either remarried (or even if one married for the first time), both had mutual obligations and privileges.

Jesus saw woman as being first and foremost an individual: a unique person (Matt. 22:23-30; cf. Mark 12:18-27, Luke 20:27-28). Woman is accorded a soul, and she had an inalienable right to be with him in heaven (Matt. 12:46-50; cf. Mark 3:31-35; Luke 8:19-21, and 11:27-28).

Unlike the Jews, and later the early Christian men, Jesus was not afraid of women or their physiology. He not only approached women, but talked with women, and healed women (Mark 1:29-31; cf. Matt. 8:14-15; Luke 4: 38-39,, where Jesus heals Peter's mother-in-law). He rejected the Jewish concept that an "issue of blood" made a woman unclean (Mark 5:24-34; cf. Matt. 9:18-26; Luke 8:40-56). Jesus even healed a woman on the Sabbath, and called her a *"daughter* of Abraham" (Luke 19:9)—totally outside of the standard of Hebrew and Jewish terminology which only recognized men to be "sons of the covenant" (*bnei brith*) (Luke 13:10-17).

Jesus was not a xenophobic, any more than he was anti-woman, as seen in his relationship with the Syrophoenician woman who he publicly testified had a "great faith" and cured her daughter (Matt. 15:21-28). His concern for her was as great as his was for other women: be they widows (Luke 2:36; 4:25-27; 18:1-8; and 21:1-4; Mark 12:38-44; Matt. 8:14-15; John 19:25-27), and adultresses (John 8:2-11). and public sinners (*en hamartolos*: "had a bad name" or "was a sinner", as in Luke 7:36-50). Jesus even accepted prostitutes, and promised that they would enter into his heaven (Matt. 21:23, 31-32) for the prostitute was an *exploited* woman, who nevertheless is a *person* who had the right to salvation and paradise. It is for these reasons that so many women were the first to accept the call of Jesus and follow him: Mary, the sister of Martha, was among the first to accept him while he still lived (Luke 10:38-42). Others also accepted his call and became his disciples, and went out as ministers (*diekonoun*) to others "out of their own resources" (Luke 8:1-3; cf. Mark 15:40-41; Matt. 27:55-56).

In light of the Synoptic Gospels it is impossible to ignore that women served as ministers during the life time of Jesus. All three of the Synotpic Gospels use a form of the verb *diakoneo* ("to serve" or "to minister") in describing what these women did. Never once did Jesus call them back, admonish them, or rebuke them. Never once did the Gospel writers hesitate in describing their ministry as accepted by Christ. They even ministered to Christ—and he listened:

> There were some women watching from a distance. Among them were Mary of Magdala, Mary who was the mother of James the younger and Joset, and Salome. These used to follow him and minister (*diekonoun*) to him when he was in Galilee. And there were many other women there who had come up to Jerusalem with him. (Mark 15:40-41)

> And many women were there, watching from a distance, the same women who had followed Jesus from Galilee and ministered (*diakonousai*) to him. Among them were Mary of Magdala, Mary the mother of James and Joseph, and the mother of Zebedee's sons. (Matt. 27:55-56).

The importance of these female disciples is made even more clear in the extracanonical documents, such as the *Sophia Jesu Christi*, probably written during the second century *anno Domini*; it puts seven holy women on par with the twelve male followers which today's theologians term to be Christ's disciples.[3] The same is the substance of the account of Salome and Jesus in the Gospel of Thomas.[4] Even the canonical Gospels suggest this, especially in the case of Mary of Magdala (Magdalene; she appears twelve times alone in the list of those who witnessed and/or testified to the resurrection of Christ in the four Gospels; there is no valid reason to identify her with the sinful woman of Luke 7:37-50, or Mary of Bethany, and is always at the head of the list of those who ministered to Jesus during his life time). She was a woman sent by Jesus as his emissary (*apostellein*) to the male apostles (John 20:17), and then to the rest of the world she would reach[4] for which she would be called "the apostle to the apostles" by the acerbic Bernard of Clairvaux in the twelfth century.[5]

Even the reputed woman-hating Paul was open to admit that women were most active and ambitious for the faith in the ministry needs of the new Church.[6] This was a mainstay for the early Church which could not be sacrificed, for not only did women help spread the news of Christ's life, passion, death, and resurrection, but women were among the first to receive and use the gift of prophecy to convert others to Christ:

ΔΙΟΔΕΥΣΑΝΤΕΣ δὲ τὴν Ἀμφί-
πολιν καὶ τὴν Ἀπολλωνίαν ἦλθον εἰς
Θεσσαλονίκην, ὅπου ἦν συναγωγὴ τῶν
Ἰουδαίων. Κατὰ δὲ τὸ εἰωθὸς τῷ
Παύλῳ εἰσῆλθεν πρὸς αὐτούς, καὶ ἐπὶ
σάββατα τρία διελέξατο αὐτοῖς ἀπὸ
τῶν γραφῶν, Διανοίγων καὶ παρα-
τιθέμενος ὅτι τὸν Χριστὸν ἔδει παθεῖν
καὶ ἀναστῆναι ἐκ νεκρῶν, καὶ ὅτι
οὗτός ἐστιν Χριστὸς Ἰησοῦς, ὃν ἐγὼ
καταγγέλλω ὑμῖν. Καί τινες ἐξ
αὐτῶν ἐπείσθησαν καὶ προσεκληρώθησαν τῷ. Παύλῳ καὶ τῷ Σίλᾳ, τῶν
τε σεβομένων Ἑλλήνων πλῆθος πολύ,
γυναικῶν τε τῶν πρώτων οὐκ ὀλίγαι.

("Now when they had passed through Amphipolis and Apollonia, they came to Thessalonica, where there was a synagogue of the Jews. And, Paul, as was his custom, went into them, and [for] three sabbath days discussed scripture with them, arguing that Christ must have suffered and risen from the dead, claiming "this Jesus which I tell you about is the annointed one". Some of those [who heard] believed and followed Paul and Silas; they were a great number, these holy Greeks, and many were

important women. Acts 17:4) Even the Syriac is the same
in content and import:

ܡܸܢܗܘܿܢ ܩܢܘ ܢܵܩܦܘ ܘܗܵܒܘܿ ܟܹܐܦܘܼܣ

ܘܓܸܠܒܹܐ . ܘܡܸ‍ܢ ܢܹܫܹ̈ܐ ܢܵܦܹ̈ܬܵܐ

ܐܸܢܹ̈ܝܢ ܕܡܸܫܠܹ̈ܐ ܗܘܘ ܡܸܢ ܓܘ ܐܹܕܬܵܐ .

ܘܗܵܘ ܬܩܵܐ ܢܡ̈ܝܓܹ̈ܐ ܠܵܐ ܐܝܚ̈ܕܵܢܹܐ .

Some of the Apostle's daughters even accepted the
ministerial call, as was the case with Phillip's daughters
who became numbered among the first prophetesses in the
early Church.[7] Paul saluted these women,[8] and later
Church historians wrote about them.[9] These were special
women: women who opened their homes to travelling
missionaries, took in the homeless and sick, held meetings
to teach non-Christians the Christian message, and brought
discipline to the early Christian community. For this reason the male Apostles listed their names before their husbands—a marked sign of their importance since it was not
only uncustomary to list a woman before a man, but a
considered insult to the dignity of the male and his *gens*.[10]

NOTES

[1]See Phyllis Bird, "Images of Woman in the Old Testament,"
in *Religion and Sexism*, ed. Rosemary Radford Ruether (New York,
1974), pp. 41-88; cf. my *Woman in ancient Israel under the Torah
and Talmud*, for additional commentary.

[2]Much of this Gospel is a variation on the four traditionally
accepted Gospels; see *New Testament Apocrypha*, vol. 1, pp. 289-
290.

[3]*Ibid.*, p. 246.

[4]*Ibid.*, p. 298.

[5]Jean-Paul Migne, ed.. *Patrologia cursus completus . . . serie
Latina* (Paris) vol. 183, col. 1148; cf. *ibid.*, vol. 112, cols. 1474B-
1475A.

[6]Phil. 4:3. The first woman to be called a prophet (*prophetis*) was "Anna the daughter of Phanuel, of the tribe of Asher. She was well on in years. . . . She came by just at that moment [when Jesus entered the Temple] and began to praise God; and she spoke of the child to all who looked forward to the deliverance of Jerusalem" (Luke 2:36-38). Jesus' aunt Elizabeth was also considered a prophet by the Gospel writers, for she foretold of Mary's conception (Luke 1:41-45), to which Mary, the Mother of Jesus responded with the famed "Magnificat", which even Pope Paul VI in *marialis Cultus*, 37, acknowledged as prophetic. Women numbered among those at Pentecost who received the gift of prophecy: "They went to the upper room. . . .All these joined in continuous prayer, together with several women, including Mary the mother of Jesus. . . . When Pentecost day came around, they had all met in one room, when suddenly they heard what sounded like a powerful wind from heaven, the noise of which filled the entire house in which they were sitting; and something appeared to them that seemed like tongues of fire; these separated and came to rest on the head of each of them. They were *all* filled with the Holy Spirit and began to speak foreign languages as the Spirit gave them the gift of speech." (Acts 1:13-14, and 2:1-4).

[7]"The end of our voyage from Tyre came when we landed at Ptolemais where we greeted the faithful and stayed for a day with them. The next day we left and came to Caesarea. Here we called on Phillip the evangelist, one of the Seven, and stayed with him. He had four virgin daughters who were prophets." (Acts 21:7-9).

[8]Acts 13:50; cf. I Cor. 11:4-5. Paul acknowledges the existence and role of women as prophetesses, requiring them only to have their heads covered—as rabbi do when reading the Torah.

[9]Eusebius of Caesarea (A.D. 260-340), wrote before A.D. 303, in the *Ecclesiastical History* (III.31): "The date of John's death has also been roughly figured [or, fixed] ; the place where his mortal remains lie can be gathered from a letter of Polycrates, Bishop of Ephesus [present day Turkey], to [Pope] Victor [I, pontiff A.D. 189-198] Bishop of Rome. In it he refers not only to John but to Philip the Apostle and Philip's daughters as well: "In Asia great luminaries sleep who shall rise again on the last day, the day of the Lord's advent, when He is coming with glory from heaven, and shall search out all His saints—such as Philip, one of the twelve apostles, who sleeps in Hierapolis with two of his daughters, who remained unmarried to the end of their days, while his other daughter lived in the Holy Spirit and rests in Ephesus." So much Polycrates tells us about their deaths. And in the *Dialogue* of Gaius of whom I spoke a little while ago, Proclus, with whom he was disputing, speaks thus about the deaths of Philip and his daughters, in agreement with the foregoing account: "After him there were four women prophets at Hierapolis in Asia, daughters of Philip. Their grave is there, as is their father's." That is Gaius' account. Luke in the Acts of the Apostles refers to Philip's daughters as then living with their father at Caesarea in Judea and endowed with the prophetic gift."

[10]Acts 12:12, and 16:14-15, 40; Romans 16:3, 5 (and see Chapter Four, immediately following); I cor. 10:1, and 16:15, 17, 19; Col. 4:15. Some of these women were even numbered as apostles; Paul heralds Junia as an "outstanding apostle" (*apostolos*): "Greetings. . . to those outstanding *apostles* Andronicus and *Junia*, my compatriots and fellow prisoners who became Christians before me." (Romans 16:6-8; and see my discussion below). Even the virulent misogynist John Chrysostom, fourth-century bishop of Constantinople, saluted Junia as an apostle (see *The Homilies of St. John Chrysostom*, in the *Nicene and Post-Nicene Fathers* series I, vol. 11, p. 55 (Grand Rapids, MI, 1956). The Council of Nicea (A.D. 325) acknowledged this to be the precedent for women to be clerics, since they came from the source of deaconesses: "Likewise, however, both deaconesses (*diakonisson*) and in general all those who are numbered among the clergy [*kanoni* in the Greek, *clericos* in the Latin] should retain the same form." (J.D. Mansi, *Sacrorum conciliorum nova et amplissa collectio* (Florence, 1757-1798), vol. 2, pp. 676ff. Even that great woman-hater Tertullian acknowledged it (*Patrologia Latina*, vol. 2, col. 978).

Chapter Five
Women & the Establishment of the Church

The first two chapters of the record of the *Acts of the Apostles* makes it abundantly clear that women were (1) numbered among the Apostles (Acts 1:14 οὗτοι πάντες ἦσαν προσκαρτεροῦντες ὁμοθυμαδὸν τῇ προσευχῇ σὺν γυναιξὶ καὶ Μαρία τῇ μητρὶ τοῦ Ἰησοῦ καὶ σὺν τοῖς ἀδελφοῖς αὐτοῦ), and (2) that women—*along with men*—received the gift of languages and the ordination to the priesthood of Jesus in the descent of the Holy Spirit which presented a physical demonstration and testimony of itself in the form of tongues of fire (or illumination) which came to rest on the heads of *all* who were meeting in the Upper Room, as described by Acts 1:14: (Καὶ ἐν συμπληροῦσθαι τὴν ἡμέραν τῆς Πεντηκοστῆς ἦσαν πάντες ὁμοῦ ἐπὶ τὸ αὐτά καὶ ἐγέκετο ἄφνω ἐκ τοῦ οὐρανοῦ ἦχος ὥσπερ φερομένης πνοῆς βιαίας καὶ ἐπλήρωσεν ὅλον τὸν οἶκον οὗ ἦσαν καθήμανοι καὶ ὤφθησαν αὐτοῖς διαμεριζόμεναι γλῶσσαι ὡσει πυρός καὶ ἐκάθισεν ἐφ ἕνα ἕκαστον αὐτῶν. καὶ ἐπλήσθησαν πάντες Πνεύματος Ἁγίου καὶ ἤρξαντο λαλεῖν ἑτέραις γλώσσαις καθὼς τὸ Πνεῦμα ἐδίδου ἀποφθέγγεσθαι αὐτοῖς Acts 2:1-4).

If the traditional interpretation of the founding of the Christian church on the resurrection of Jesus Christ (I Cor. 15:12-19) is to be upheld, and, at the same time, that the ministry of the name and message of Jesus came with the descent of the Holy Spirit (Acts 2:1-4) is to be continued, then it is nonsense to argue against women being numbered among those commissioned and ordained to the ministry (*e.g.* work) of Jesus. Furthermore, since it was women who carried the news of Jesus resurrection to men (Matt. 28:1f; Mk. 16:1-8; Lk. 24:1-2; Jn. 20:1-3), the very knowledge of the foundation of the Church on the resurrection of Jesus would not have been known, and possibly the male disciples would not have met in the Upper Room. The fact that the male disciples doubted the word of the women concerning the resurrection of Jesus shows that women were more willing to accept the fullness of Christ than were men, had greater faith, and were more willing to spread the *gospel* (good news) of his resurrection which completed the Old Testament prescription for the messiah, and at the same time made his faith a living faith. The fact that not only did the male disciples doubt the initial message, but also that only one (or at best two) male disciples returned with the women to the empty tomb, again demonstrates their reluctance to accept the testimony of women (quite in keeping with the cultural restraints that they had labored and lived under as children and as men, as did so many other generations of socially conditioned-enslaved men).

But there was a turning point somewhere in this male chauvinism and social conditioning, for women were admitted to the Upper Room, they did commune as equals with the men in the Upper Room, and they were present and equal recipients of the Holy Spirit. Thus in every sense of the word, women were *Apostles* of Christ—and as equal in nature and extent as Sts. Peter and Paul: St. Peter who had been among the first of the original twelve called, and St. Paul (Saul of Tarsus) who had been among the earliest persecutors of the early Christians, who was not called until he was thrown off of his horse.

Women not only were in the Upper Room and received the descent (or ordination) of the Holy Spirit, but were also among the very earliest converts to the Christian faith: "And the number of men and *women* who came to believe in the Lord increased steadily" (Acts 5:14). That there were a large number of women converts to Christianity in Palestine is reflected in the accounts of their persecution by Saul of Tarsus: "Saul then worked for the total destruction of the Church, he went from house to house arresting both men and *women* and sending them to prison" (Acts 8:3 Σαῦλος δὲ ἐλμαίνετο τὴν ἐκκλησίαν κατὰ τοὺς οἴκους εἰσπορευόμενος σύρων τε ἄνδρας καὶ γυναῖκας παρεδίδου εἰς φυλακήν). If women had not been "great in numbers" among the converts to the Christian message, they would not have been mentioned, for it was not yet the religious custom to mention women in religious tracts.

The fact that Saul (St. Paul) continued his persecutions of men *and women* even outside of Palestine, confirms the fact that the numbers of converts was growing, and, too, that women were persecuted singularly and in number, shows how great the initial movement was feared to be. To stop this "threat" the Christians supposedly presented, Saul traveled to Syria to arrest the "infidels":

"Meanwhile Saul was still breathing threats to slaughter the Lord's disciples. He had gone to the high priest and asked for letters addressed to the synagogues in Damascus, that would authorize him to arrest and take to Jerusalem any followers of the Way, men *or women*, that he could find.

Ὁ δὲ Σαῦλος ἔτι ἐμπνέων ἀπειλῆς καὶ φόνου εἰς τοὺς μαθητὰς τοῦ Κυρίου προσελθὼν τῶ ἀρχιερεῖ ἠτήσατο παρ' αὐτοῦ ἐπιστολὰς εἰς Δαμασκόν πρὸς τὰς συναγωγὰς ὅπως ἐάν τινας εὕρη τῆς ὁδοῦ ὄντας ἄνδας τε καὶ γυναῖκας δεδεμένους ἀγάγη εἰς Ἰερουσαλήμ

(Acts 9:1-2), which he, himself, confessed:

I even persecuted this Way to the death, and sent *women* as well as men to prison in chains, as the high priest and the whole council of elders can testify.

...ὃς ταύτην τὴν ὁδὸν ἐδίωξα ἄχρι θανάτου δεσμεύων καὶ παραδιδοὺς εἰς φυλακὰς ἄνδρας τε καὶ γυναῖκας ὡς καὶ ὁ ἀργιερεὺς μαρτυρεῖ μοι καὶ πᾶν τὸ πρεσβυτέριθν· παρ' ὧν καὶ ἐπιστολὰς δεξάμενος πρὸς τοὺς ἀδελφοὺς εἰς Δαμασκὸν ἐπορευόμην, ἄξων καὶ τοὺς ἐκεῖσε ὄντας δεδεμένους εἰς Ἰερουσαλήμ ἵνα τιμωρηθωσιν

(Acts 22:4-5).

Because of his bitter attacks on women, Saul, following his conversion to Christ (which he demonstrated by using the name Paul), preached especially to women. At the Roman colony of Philippi he preached, in fact, to a congregation made up *exclusively* of women (Acts 16:13). The records say nothing about this congregation having any men in attendance or membership!

One of the women in the congregation of Philippi

was Lydia. She was the first "European" convert to the faith of Jesus. There are many unique aspects about this woman—which gives account of some of the lot of women in this age. We do know for a fact (1), that she was a believer in a deity ("a God-worshipper"); (2) she was a businessperson engaged in a trade ("was in the purple-dye trade") which was quite lucrative at the time, therefore she was a woman of means, and since it was her trade, she was certainly a woman of initiative, ambition, drive, and self-determination. (3) Lydia was a person who hungered for knowledge, she did not accept the tradition that women were to be unlearned, and thus "she listened to us"—a criteria Jesus had set down when he admonished Martha who wished him to rebuke Mary who had sat at his feet as a student eager to learn. (4) She thought about what had been said, and after considering the merits of the sermon, decided to adopt the new faith for herself and her household (another indication of her great means) "She listened to us. . . [and] After she and her household had been baptised". She was (5) a generous person, and "sent us an invitation: 'If you really think me [to be] a true believer in the Lord,' she said, 'come and stay with us'." And, last of all, she was a determined woman who would not accept refusals on anything she had set her mind to: "and she would take no refusal.":

One of these women was called Lydia, a God-worshipper, who was from the town of Thyatira and was in the purple-dye trade. She listened to us, and the Lord opened her heart to accept what Paul was saying. After she and her household had been baptised she sent us an invitation: "If you really think me a true believer in the Lord," she said, "come and stay with us"; and she would take no refusal.

καὶ τις γυκὴ ὀνοματι Λυδία πορφτρόπωλις πόλεως Θυατείρων σεβομένη τὸν Θεόν ἤκουεν· ἧς ὁ Κύριος διήνοιξε τὴν καρδίαν προσέχειν τοῖς λαλουμένοις ὑπὸ τοῦ Παύλος ὡς δὲ ἐβαπτίσθη καὶ ὁ οἶκος αὐτῆς παρεικάλεσε λέγουσα. Εἰ κεκρίκατέ με πιστὴν τῶ Κυρίω εἶναι εἰσελθόντες εἰς τὸν οἶκόν μου μείνατε και παρεβιάσατο ἡμᾶς...

(Acts 16:14-15).

Lydia was not the only woman to come to the Christian community from an upper-class Gentile background. Many Greek women also came: "And some of them were persuaded and joined Paul and Silas, as did a great many of the devout Greeks and *not a few of the leading women* (καί τινες ἐξ αὐτῶν ἐπείσθησαν καὶ προσεκληρώθησαν τῶ Παύλω καὶ τῶ Σίλα τῶν τε σεβομένων Ἑλλήνων πολὺ πλῆθος γυναικῶν τε τῶν πρώτων οὐκ ὀλίγαι Acts 17:4) of Thessalonica, at Beroea, where the women were listed first—*before* men— a marked indication of their importance: "Many of them therefore believed, with *not a few Greek women of high standing* as well as men (πολλοὶ μὲν οὖν ἐξ αὐτῶν ἐπίστευσαν καὶ τῶν Ἑλληνίδων γυναικῶν τῶν εὐοχημόνων καὶ ἀνδρῶν οὐκ ὀλίγοι Acts 17:12), and in Athens, where a particular woman, Damaris, is singled out for special recorded recognition (Acts 17:34).

Women were not only converts to early Christianity, but also workers with Paul and by themselves in spreading the message of Jesus. They were evangelists, and their numbers included Chloe (I Cor. 1:11), Aquila and Prisca, and Claudia (II Tim. 4:19, 21; Romans 16:1; cp. Acts 18: 2), Phoebe, who was a recognized deacon (*diakonon*) in the church (Romans 16:1) in Cenchreae; Julia, Nereus' sister, and Olympas (Romans 16:15; and seven other women), Mary, Tryphaena and her sister Tryphosa (Romans 16:6, 12), Persis (Romans 16:11-12), and the mother of Rufus (Romans 16:13).[1]

Paul testifies that these women "worked hard in the Lord." (Romans 16:12). Junia, Paul proclaimed, was his compatriot and fellow prisoner, who became a Christian even before he did (Romans 16:7). Phoebe was a ruler (deacon) of the Church, who had even ruled over him "for she has been a ruler over many, indeed over me" (Romans 16:1-2 Συνίστημι δὲ ὑμῖν Φοίβην τὴν ἀδελφὴν ἡμῶν οὖσαν διάκονον τῆς ἐκκλσίας τῆς ἐν Κεγχρεαῖς ἵνα αὐτὴν προσδέξησθε ἐν Κυρίω ἀξίωστῶν ἁγίων καὶ παραστῆτε αὐτῇ ἐν ὦ ἀν ὑμῶν χρήζη πράγματι καὶ γὰρ αὐτὴ προστάτις πολλων ἐγενήθη καὶ ἐμοῦ αὐτοῦ).[2]

Eudoia and Syntyche "struggled" with Paul in spreading the gospel (Phil. 4:2). Eudoia and Syntyche had some major disagreement which threatened the fabric of the Church 'in Philippi; that the two were critical to the church in Philippi and its development can be seen in Paul's extra zeal in urging them to patch up their differences, turning to Eudoia with the special acknowledgement that she was "my dependable worker" (Phil. 4: 3).

Women sometimes were the source of Paul's knowledge of what was occurring in the churches. Chloe was the individual to tell Paul of troubles in the church at Corinth (I Cor. 1:11). This is, at the same time, an indication that women were administrators as well as ministers (e.g. Phoebe, in Romans 16:1-2; Apphia, in Philem 1-2; Aquila and Prisca, in Romans 16:3, 5, and I Cor. 16:19; cp. Acts 18:1-3, Prisca is here called Priscilla; some theologians feel that Priscilla/Prisca is the author of the Epistle to the Hebrews[3]).

That women in the Apostolic Age were ministers can be seen in a textual comparison of the various scriptures. Christ, himself, sanctified the term diakonos when he applied it not only to those who labored with him, but to his own mission on earth (Romans 15:8). The context of the expression is the same for both men and women, as can be seen in the reference to the diaconate of Apollos (I Cor. 3:5), and the diaconate of Phoebe (Romans 16:1). In both cases the term/word is identical to that which Paul applies to himself, as well (I Cor. 3:5; Ephes. 3:7; Col. 1:23).

St. Paul's "adversion" to women needs to be carefully scrutinized. The critical passages[4] most probably are later additions, spurious in nature and of doubtful origin.[5] The most damning reference is the passage in I Corinthians 11: 2-6, which subordinates the wife to her husband. This passage requires woman (gyne) to be veiled when she prophesies and prays, while the man is forbidden to wear a head covering or to have long hair at any time when he prays or prophesies. The key to this passage, if it is authentic, is that it ties woman into an ossified and staid hierarchy with woman placed below man. However, I seriously doubt its authenticity. At best, I must argue, it must be interpreted broadly and not closedly literally. The tenth verse of I Corinthians actually reads "the woman *ought* to have a sign of *submission (exousia)* on her head". The Greek word *exousia* has a basic and pristine meaning of power or freedom of action. It does *not* mean "submission"—as it is translated in so many English editions, in the sense or definition of being less than, or enslaved to: instead it is a statement that woman *as well as man* is subject to God and for God. *Exousia* is a term for the symbol of woman submitting herself to God—in a manner tantamount to the "veil" worn by the rabbis when reading the Torah; in this case it is a statement that she has rabbinical or teaching powers when she is in an assembly of the faithful *when* her head *may be* covered. At the same time the text does not command it to be *always* covered when she prays and prophesies, for the text uses the phrase "the woman *ought* to have". Therefore, instead of this being a negative statement suppressing woman, it should be read and understood as a positive statement elevating woman to the rabbinical power and position of teacher, as well as giving entrance to her to join with men in ruling and ministering the church: *dia tous angelous* ("in the company of angels").[6]

That the old fashioned injunction against women participating in the religious services and observances must be defined according to Paul's own assunderation of the prohibitive code, and his entonement that woman and man are equals: "Moreover, neither is woman apart from man, nor man apart from woman in the Lord; just as woman is out of man, thus also man is out of woman, and all things are come from God" (I Cor. 11:11-12). Since all things are equal before God, and since God does not recognize sexual differences, women, therefore, are as welcome to the ministry—teaching and ruling—as are men! This is the main theme in the New Testament Apocrypha.[7]

Women were a part of the growing Church. Paul argues that women were responsible for the growth of the Church (Romans 16:1-2; Col. 4:15; Philem 1-2; Acts 18:

18-19f). Extracanonical scriptures also attest to the significance women played in the founding of the early primi-
tive church. Ignatius of Antioch, in his famous *Address to
the Romans*[8] applauds the number and zeal of women
converts to the faith of Christ. He testifies that women,
in fact, were more ambitious for the faith, spreading the
gospel of the resurrection of Jesus, and proselyting among
all peoples moreso than could be acclaimed of male converts. Those women who were "wound up in the faith"
rejected the tradition as expounded by male Jews on
the inferiority of women ("Praised be God that he has not
created me a Gentile! Praise be God that he has not created me a woman! Praise be God that he has not created me
a slave!"—*Tosephta Berakhoth* 7, 18), and capitalized on
the liberating statement of Paul ("All [are] baptised in
Christ, you have all clothed yourselves in Christ, and there
are no more distinctions between Jew and Greek, slave and
free, male and female, but all of you are one in Christ
Jesus"—Gal. 2:27-28). At the same time this emancipation
did, certainly, dissuade some Jews from joining the new
movement, for it was outside of the mainstream of their
tradition and thought. Thus, the majority of the new
converts grew from the ranks of the Gentiles, and especially Gentile women.[9]

The new liberation did have additional side effects.
Some women, in jubilation over the new freedom,
attempted to abolish all sexual distinctions, so as to create
heaven on earth—an aspiration both unknown, incompre-
hensible, and unwelcome among men.[10] This undoubtedly spurred Silvanus (or Silas), a frequent companion of
Paul (cf. I Pet. 5:12), to write out a set of rules for women
stratifying them to the chains of yesteryear (Eph. 5:21-33;
Col. 3:18, Titus 2:3-9; I Pet. 3:1-7). The author of these
statements, in direct opposition to the teachings of Jesus
and the writings of Paul, reaffirms the Hellenistic morality
placed on women before the liberation of Jesus had been
ennunciated. This anti-Christian comment is exceeded only
by the radical departure from the theme of Christ as
found in the second century writing by the writer of I
Timothy 2:9-15, which castigates woman's beauty—while

saying nothing about the physical appearance of men. This comment is a direct refutation of the theme of Paul and in total conflict with his liberating declaration of equality, as found in Col. 3:11. This offending line in Timothy is far more in tune with the misogynistic writings of apostate Tertullian, in his *De Baptismo* (17:4), who questioned whether or not Paul ever did commission women to preach and teach, lamenting the example of Thelca—who was listed as a saint by the Roman Catholic Church—until 1969!

Not only is I Timothy 2:9-15 an unnecessary and illogical offense to the basic Christian message, and in direct opposition to the teachings of Paul, it is outside the main apostolic view of women as found in the Gospels, whose authorship is still in debate. The Gospel of Matthew, written sometime after 70 A.D., rejects the concept of woman as being only a sex object. The author(s) of this work, instead, registers a strong protest against male exploitation of women: women no longer are singularly guilty of adultery, but men are considered equally responsible (Matt. 5:27-28), and, again, Christ witnesses that in heaven there is no sexual distinction or qualifier (Matt. 5:28-31). Whereas Jewish tradition characterized woman as foolish, the author(s) of Matthew rejects this fallacy, and details the wisdom of even the common woman (Matt. 25:1-13), again graphing the new theology as declared by Jesus on the quality and equality of the sexes. For those men who still held out against the company of women, this author, or these authors, elevate women to another position of prominence, relating how it was primarily women and children who made up the host whom Christ fed when he gave his sermon on the Mount (whereas in the Marcian text, the account merely notes that Christ fed five thousand; Mk. 6:44), and then embellishes this account with the jeweled statement noting that there were certain women in this congregation who had faith greater than that which could be discovered in men (Matt. 15:21-28). All of this liberation of women culminates in the final glory when the gospel writer(s) likens God's people to a daughter: one who is compassionate, tender, believing, and faithful—"even unto death." (Matt. 21:5).

The Gospel of Matthew brings this equality in to the public arena, and goes so far as to take it beyond the Jewish sector. The strength of women is made public in the writer(s) account of the confrontation between Pilate and his wife. It is the Roman governor's wife who attempts to change his mind concerning the execution of Christ. The fact that she spoke up and attempted to counsel her husband is not as remarkable as the fact that the writer(s) chose to record this incident and make it gospel. This magnificent line is a direct rejection of the misogynistic line in I Timothy which enslaves and reduces women to wrongfully be subordinate to men: "I permit no woman to teach or have authority over men...." What is even more unique about this passage in Matthew (27:19ff), is that Pilate rejects his wife's sound advise, listens to his male counsel and surrenders his own principles and morality when he is threatened with the loss of his job, and the loss of favor with the emperor.

Because of Pilate's own fear of the intelligence of woman, he permitted the consignment of Christ to the cross. Because of this execution the Christian message was completed. But its fullness was not known until women carried the news of the empty tomb to men who continued to doubt—still afraid of the wisdom of women (Matt. 28:10f).

What is especially noteworthy in Matthew is the fact that women are not played down or demoted in the words of Christ. Those negative aspects found in Matthew against women come from the Jewish male population, or those Gentile elements which traditionally were anti-woman. The statements of Christ, and record of the life of Christ as found in Matthew remains positive in it dealing with women.

This same positive attitude and testimony towards women is found in the Marcian Gospel. Its' author(s) gives prominence and preeminence to women in at least a dozen major situations. Mary, the mother of

Jesus, is treated with respect, and is given significant attention (3:31-35, 6.1-6, 15:40 and 47, 16:1[11]). Christ is more than "dutiful"–he is obedient.

In a similar manner Christ treats other women. Thus he attends the mother of Simon bar Jonas (Peter), cures her of a fever, and then allows her to minister to him (here the term "minister" is broad and encompassing, thus we cannot tell exactly what all she did). What is significant about this passage is that Jesus did not have to seclude himself away from the woman or to seek out and to accept the ministrations of his male disciples. Here again we find Jesus' acceptance of a woman as tantamount to that of a man.

The author(s) of Mark go further. In this account Jesus continues to reject social taboos. Here we read of Christ calling the woman afflicted with a hemorrhage of blood "daughter"–while his society had cast her out, expelling her as "one unclean" (Mk. 5:34). Also, in this account, we find Jesus calling the daughter of Jairus his daughter–eventhough Jairus was a ruler of the synagogue which had rejected him and considered Jesus the enemy (Mk. 5:21f). The daughter of Jairus was, in the eyes of Jesus, no different than the Syrophoenician woman, who Jesus cared for and assisted–as if she had been Jewish and one of his immediate followers (Mk. 7:24-30).

The author(s) of Mark gives to the reader an insight as to the final struggle between the sexes. It is a proto-promise of the demise of the double-standard. This future is found in the bud of Christ's concept of divorce, which flowers in a most spectacular way, for Christ pulls the strangling weeds of decadent custom and prohibitions and segregation of the sexes out of the fertile earth surrounding the stem of humanity, allowing it to grow in richness and hardiness.

Whereas man in the past had been allowed to divorce his wife, Christ reversed the coin of contemporary consciousness, and told his listeners that neither party had the right to divorce, and that both parties in a marriage had responsibilities to the other. Divorce, according to Christ, is not a viable alternative to settling difficulties and differences. Communication, love and the acceptance of equality between the parties involved is the only way to permanence, and emotional, psychological, and affectional growth. The author(s) of Mark record Christ saying, "The man who divorces his wife and marries another is guilty of adultery against her. And if a woman divorces her husband and marries another, she is guilty of adultery, too." (Mk.10:11-12).

This same sense of equality permeates the writings found under the title of the Gospel According to Luke. In this tract (or set of tracts), we find women equally occupying a place of prominence. Here specific women are named, and their livelihoods, functions, and gifts are detailed. Elizabeth, the aunt of Jesus, is highlighted in the narrative, as is the prophet Anna who "never left the Temple," but served "God night and day with fasting and prayer" It was she who first, among those bound to the earth "spoke of the child to all who looked forward to the deliverance of Jerusalem" (Lk. 2:36-38).

This deliverance of Jersualem by Jesus was noted further in the text by the *diekonoun* of Jesus, who are ennumerated and named: "Mary surnamed the Magdalene, from whom seven demons had gone out, Joanna the wife of Herod's steward Chuza, Susanna, and several others [women] who ministered (*diekonoun*) to them out of their own resources" (Lk. 8:1-3). This entire epic of deliverance even begins with women (beginning with the birth of Jesus), and ends with women who come to the open tomb, hear the message of the resurrection, and then spread the good news to the male disciples and to the world as a whole.

There is no denigration of women in the Gospel of Luke. Nor is there any true trace of misogyny. When sexual discrimination against women appears, it is only a record of the occurences of the society in which Jesus is at that particular time, a reflection of the common attitude prevailing and suffocating all those who had not yet accepted his word emancipating them from their psychological chains.

Little else can be said about the Gospel of Luke. Its author(s) follow, in nearly every way, the pattern and message as left by the writer(s) of Mark.[12]

What distinguishes the Gospel of Luke from the Gospel of Mark, however, is that in this particular record we find material incorporated no where else. Elizabeth is introduced. She is brought forward as an illustration of woman's piety—a piety very real, very intense, very personal—and a piety equal to that of any man! a piety which most Jewish males denied was possible of a woman (Lk. 1:1-6ff).

At that same time, it is in the Gospel of Luke that we find the "miraculous conception." It is stressed as a "divine love" by God for humankind that was expressed and sent to earth through a woman—not a man! This, in itself, is a testimony of God's own love for woman and God's determination to use woman in divine ministry.[13]

The significance of woman is carried throughout the account known as the Gospel of Luke. Thus the forerunner of Jesus, John the Baptist, is born of a woman whose history is given—a quite uncommon occurence in the Bible. We read of how Mary, too, produced a son— eventhough she was not yet married at the time—nor, according to the written word, had she known penial intromission with a man. Even the birth is detailed, and visitors come to pay their homage to the child and to the woman.

The woman continues as a thread throughout the account. Christ's greatest compassion is for women, as found in the account of his attendance upon the widow of Nain whose son lay dead. Christ saw the bereaveds procession to the family tomb, carrying the dead son. Without hesitating, he approached, sought out the mother, and then breathed life back into the boy and returned him to his mother (Lk. 7:11-17).

Within this same account we read of Christ's relationship with other women: some of whom were considered public sinners. But in each case Christ shows them an uncommon compassion, accepts them, and rebukes those who would have him leave them alone

(Lk. 10:38-42).

Following the pattern, this same theme runs through the Gospel of John—written much later. In this record the same compassionate feeling for women is exhibited in Jesus who raised Lazarus to be returned alive to Mary and Martha (Jn. 11:1-2). At the same time the author(s) of this gospel are more guarded.[14] Women are singled out by name more exclusively. Mary of Magdala is the only one who is acknowledged to have been at the empty tomb (Jn. 20:11).

The Magdala plays a major role in this gospel. Not only is she loved by Christ, ministers to Christ, annoints Christ, sees Christ through his *passio*, but follows him to the tomb, awaits his embalming, returns to the tomb, finds the tomb empty, is heralded by two "angels" in white who announce that "he is arisen", shown the place where Jesus had laid, sent to carry the message of the resurrection to Simon Peter and "the disciple whom Jesus loved", and then went to witness for Jesus to the world, thus winning for herself the title of Apostle to the Apostles (Jn. 20; Bernard of Clairvaux, *loc. cit.*). All of her ministerial commissionings came from God the Father or Jesus, and thus has earned her a definite right to be numbered among the Apostles, along with Peter, Matthew, Mark, Luke, John, James, and the others.

NOTES

[1] See my *Woman as priest, bishop and laity in the early Catholic Church to 440 A.D.*.

[2] Cf. Migne, *Patrologia Graeca*, vol. 51, cols. 668f.

[3] Ruth Hoppin, *Priscilla, Author of the Epistle to the Hebrews* (New York: Exposition Press, 1969), cp. Migne, *Patrologia Graeca*, vol. 51, cols. 191f.

[4] See my *Woman as priest*, pp. 61ff: "Male collaboration against the female sex".

[5] Cf. Robin A. Scroggs, "Paul and the Eschatological Woman," *Journal of the American Academy of Religion* (September, 1972), p. 284.

[6] See my *Woman as priest,* p. 63; cp. William O. Walker, Jr., "1 Corinthians 11:2-16 and Paul's Views Regarding Women," *Journal of Biblical Literature* 94 no. 1 (March 1975) pp. 94-110.

[7] Stevan Davies, "The Social World of the Apocryphal Acts," unpublished dissertation (Temple University, 1978) gives a history. Cf. Acts of Paul and Thelca, *New Testament Apocrypha,* vol. 2, pp. 360-363, which delivers the significance of women, and where the women were in loud vocal support of the ministry of Thelca and women (p. 364).

[8] Migne, *Patrologia Graeca,* vol. 5, col. 6.3.

[9] *Acts of the Christian Martyrs* 8:2-10; cp. my *Woman in the age of Christian martyrs,* pp. 30ff.

[10] Gal. 3:28, *supra* Rom. 12:3-8 *infra* v. 6: *charismata kata charin:* cp. *ibid.,* 6:23.

[11] Cp. Papyrus Oxyrhnchus 1, lines 31-36, and *Gospel of Thomas* Logion 1 for correlates.

[12] G. Erdmann, *Die Vorgeschichte des Lukas- und Matthäus-Evangeliums und Vergils vierte Ekloge* (Göttingen, 1932); and see my *Woman in the Gospel of Mark Compared With the Gospel of Luke.*

[13] Frank Stagg, "The Unhindered Gospel," *Review and Expositor* 61 no. 4 (Fall, 1974), pp. 451-462.

[14] Raymond Brown, *The Gospel According to John* gives a good analysis, as does "John" by William E. Hull in *The Broadman Bible Commentary.*

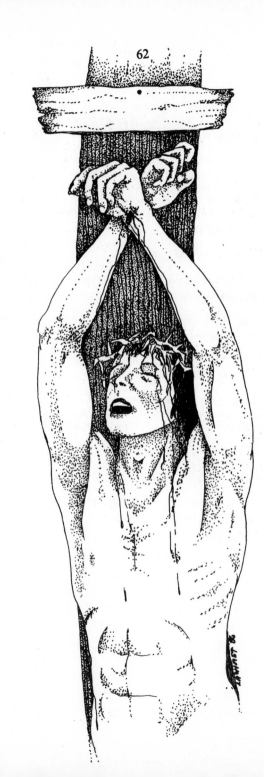

Chapter Six
The Role of Women in the Early Church

Contrary to the rhetoric of Roman pontiffs from the sixth to the twentieth century, women *did* serve as ministers: deacons, priests, and bishops in the early Catholic Church and Christian community. In general, they were called *diakonos*—a word which at that time was understood to mean "ministers" rather than "deaconesses" (*e.g.* aids to the ministers). The Latin of Pliny the Younger reads, quite clearly:

Quibus peractis morem sibi discedendi fuisse rursusque coeundi ad capiendum cibum, promiscuum tamen et innoxium; quod ipsum facere desiisse post edictum meum, quo secundum mandata tua hetaerias esse vetueram. Quo magis necessarium credidi ex duabus ancillis, quae *ministrae* dicebantur, quid esset veri et per tormenta quaerere. Sed nihil aliud inveni, quam superstitionem pravam, immodicam.

Even this practice [sharing in the *Agape*: Holy Communion], however, they had abandoned after the publication of my edict by which, according to your orders, I had forbidden political associations. I judged it so much the more necessary to extract the real truth, with the assistance of torture, from two female slaves, who were styled *ministers*, but I could discover nothing more than depraved and excessive superstition.

Pliny's accounts, similar to those left by other civil servants, record in detail how the *ministrae* "stood fast for the faith" and how their congregations "mourned the passing of their shepherds who they call also *diakonos*".[1]

The acceptance, ordination and commissioning of women to serve as *ministrae* within the early Christian community is well documented. The Greek educated legalist, St. Paul, himself greeted them as leaders of congregations, joined with them, worshiped with them, and took bread with them. The fullest statement on Paul's knowledge, understanding, and acceptance of women in the

64

clergy is found in the sixteenth chapter of Paul's Letter to
the Romans, which more than probably was delivered to
the congregation of Christians by a woman: Phoebe,
inasmuch as the first lines read:

ΣΥΝΙΣΤΗΜΙ δὲ ὑμῖν Φοίβην
τὴν ἀδελφὴν ἡμῶν, οὖσαν διάκονον τῆς
ἐκκλησίας τῆς ἐν Κεγχρεαῖς, "Ἴνα
αὐτὴν προσδέξησθε ἐν Κυρίῳ ἀξίως τῶν
ἁγίων καὶ παραστῆτε αὐτῇ ἐν ᾧ ἂν ὑμῶν
χρῄζῃ πράγματι· καὶ γὰρ αὐτὴ προστάτις πολλῶν ἐγενήθη καὶ ἐμοῦ αὐτοῦ.

ܡܰܓܥܠ ܐܢܐ ܠܟܘܢ ܕܝܢ ܠܦܘܒܐ
ܚܬܢ ܕܐܝܬܝܗ ܡܫܡܫܢܝܬܐ ܕܥܕܬܐ
ܕܩܢܟܪܐܘܣ. ܕܬܩܒܠܘܢܗ ܒܡܪܢ
ܐܝܟ ܕܙܕܩ ܠܩܕܝܫܐ. ܘܒܟܠ ܨܒܘ
ܕܒܥܝܐ ܡܢܟܘܢ ܬܩܘܡܘܢ ܠܗ. ܡܛܠ
ܕܐܦ ܗܝ ܩܝܘܡܬܐ ܗܘܬ ܠܣܓܝܐܐ ܐܦ ܠܝ.

The Latin shows that she was the minister of the church in
Cenchrea: *Commendo autem vobis Phoebem sororem
nostram quae est in ministerio ecclesiae quae est Cencris.*
This introduction, however, tells the reader even more, for
the salutation is also a letter of commendation which was a
necessity when a Christian traveled from one community
to another where that Christian would be unknown. Additionally, by selecting and sending a woman from one
church to another demonstrates Paul's awareness not only
of the existence of women, but also their determination to
carry any Christian message to any place. Third, as read in
line 2: *Ut eam suscipiatis in Domino digne sanctis et ad-
sistatis ei in quocumque negotio vestri indiguerit: etenim
ipsa quoque adsistit multis et mihi ipsi,* Phoebe *ministered*
to those who were of the Christian faith. In this case, this
line coupled with the first and the use of the title of
minister or deaconess is a clear mark that she performed
the same office in the church as men who held that rank
(cf. Phil. 1:1; I Tim. 3:8-13). This ministry was not only
caring for the poor, the sick, and the desolate, but also a
posit for an office: for she, (Paul acknowledges) had even
helped him "as she has many others." The faithful of the
church in Rome were enjoined to "receive her in the Lord,
as was it worthy of the saints." To accept Jesus was the

same as accepting one of his priests—regardless of the gender of the priest; the phrase "as was it worthy of the saints" undoubtedly meant that the new believers in Rome were to accept Phoebe as she had been accepted by Paul and the apostles, reflecting on what was owed her by them since she had already been accorded it by others. At the same time, this phrase suggests that the Roman Christians were considered "worthy" if they accepted another believer as themselves. That Phoebe was a major figure within the Christian community and not just another "helper" can be seen in the word προστατίς which means "one who presides", and is to be understood in the sense of the verb προιστηγι (cf. 12:8). This can be the only correct meaning and interpretation of this word; Paul develops into the faith with her assistance, rather than springs into a miraculous full understanding of the fine points of Christianity which makes greater sense than the ossified and chauvinistic interpretation so many male theologians give to this passage, making Paul appear as a Minerva—springing from the head of a god—fully adorned and enlightened. This interpretation gives Paul back his humanity and helps to explain Peter's difficulty with Paul's seeming lack of Christian understanding. This interpretation is further enforced and enhanced by noting the position of the name within the salutation—it places Phoebe at the citadel of the mission—a person who had the full confidence of the writer, and thereby was undoubtedly the intimate of the writer. Furthermore, because of her closeness to Paul, and because of her role in the early Church, Paul requires the Christians of Rome to give her every assistance—as deacons render priests and priests give bishops.

Unfortunately, we know nothing else of this woman (whether or not she married, was learned and wrote, or was a simple woman moved by an intense personal faith to weather all storms both natural and man-made). All we do know is that Phoebe was joined in her missionary work by other women.

Priscilla (also known as Prisca) is listed among the "other women" of the early Christian Church "who toiled" for the faith. She, too, along with Aquila, was saluted by Paul, who recognized his debt to both.

3 Ἀσπάσασθε Πρίσκαν καὶ Ἀκύλαν τοὺς συνεργούς μου ἐν Χριστῷ Ἰησοῦ, 4 Οἵτινες ὑπὲρ τῆς ψυχῆς μου τὸν ἑαυτῶν τράχηλον ὑπέθηκαν, οἷς οὐκ ἐγὼ μόνος εὐχαριστῶ ἀλλὰ καὶ πᾶσαι αἱ ἐκκλησίαι τῶν ἐθνῶν, 5 Καὶ τὴν κατ' οἶκον αὐτῶν ἐκκλησίαν. Ἀσπάσασθε Ἐπαινετὸν τὸν ἀγαπητόν μου, ὅς ἐστιν ἀπαρχὴ τῆς Ἀσίας εἰς Χριστόν. 6 Ἀσπάσασθε Μαριάμ, ἥτις πολλὰ ἐκοπίασεν εἰς ὑμᾶς. 7 Ἀσπάσασθε Ἀνδρόνικον καὶ Ἰουνίαν τοὺς συγγενεῖς μου καὶ συναιχμαλώτους μου, οἵτινές εἰσιν ἐπίσημοι ἐν τοῖς ἀποστόλοις, οἳ καὶ πρὸ ἐμοῦ γέγοναν ἐν Χριστῷ. 8 Ἀσπάσασθε Ἀμπλίατον τὸν ἀγαπητόν μου ἐν Κυρίῳ. 9 Ἀσπάσασθε Οὐρβανὸν τὸν συνεργὸν ἡμῶν ἐν Χριστῷ καὶ Στάχυν τὸν ἀγαπητόν μου. 10 Ἀσπάσασθε Ἀπελλῆν τὸν δόκιμον ἐν Χριστῷ. Ἀσπάσασθε τοὺς ἐκ τῶν Ἀριστοβούλου. 11 Ἀσπάσασθε Ἡρωδίωνα τὸν συγγενῆ μου. Ἀσπάσασθε τοὺς ἐκ τῶν Ναρκίσσου τοὺς ὄντας ἐν Κυρίῳ.

Paul met Priscilla and Aquila at Corinth (Acts 18:2), where they gave him shelter. Later they went with Paul to

Ephesus (Acts 18:18-19). While Paul continued his travels Priscilla and Aquila remained behind to teach Apollo the fundamentals of Christianity (Acts 18:26). By the time Paul wrote his letter to the Roman congregation they had returned to their native land (Romans 1:4), since the Emperor Claudius had died and his decrees against the Christians were no longer in effect for various reasons.

Paul remembered Priscilla and Aquila long after he parted company with them in Ephesus (cf. I Cor. 16:19; II Tim. 4:19). He had great respect for both, and saw each as his equal, calling them "fellow-workers in Christ Jesus" (*Salutate Priscam et Aquilam adjutores meos in Christo Jesu*), not only because they had risked their lives to save his (*qui pro anima mea suas cervices subposuerunt*) but because they worked hard for the continuance and further-ance of the Church (*quibus non solu ego gratias ago sed et cunctae ecclesiae gentium*). Not only did Priscilla and Aquila work for the Church universal and the church of Rome, but even gave it the physical shelter of their own home (*et domesticam eorum ecclesiam*). An English trans-ation of the Greek would read:

Greet Priscilla and Aquila who are my helpers in Jesus Christ, for they have risked their lives to save my life, for which not only do I render gratitude, but so,too do all the Churches of the Gen-tiles.

3 Ἀσπάσασθε Πρίσκαν καὶ Ἀκύλαν τοὺς συνεργούς μου ἐν Χριστῷ Ἰησοῦ, 4 Οἵτινες ὑπὲρ τῆς ψυχῆς μου τὸν ἑαυ-τῶν τράχηλον ὑπέθηκαν, οἷς οὐκ ἐγὼ μόνος εὐχαριστῶ ἀλλὰ καὶ πᾶσαι αἱ ἐκκλησίαι τῶν ἐθνῶν, 5 Καὶ τὴν κατ᾽ οἶκον αὐτῶν ἐκκλησίαν.

Again, we have clear evidence of the contribution a woman (Priscilla) made to the Church. Not only did a woman save Paul's life, but ministered: to Apollo and to the church in Rome. The fact that she invited the embryo community of Christians in Rome to use her home as a meeting place shows how firm she was in her faith and her willingness to suffer for it, for giving quarters to a banned sect could sound one's own death peal. As to whether or not the house of Priscilla and Aquilla was used by all of the Christian community of Rome is but speculation. Although it is difficult to imagine that there was but a single community of Christians in Rome, no where in this letter of Paul do we read of other congregations in Rome existing or meeting outside of Priscilla's home. To suggest, as some theological commentators have, that the city of Rome must be viewed similar to the city of Ephesus, as based on I Cor. 16:19, is presuming too much. There is *no* scriptural foundation to support the often given argument that there were *churches* in Rome—the text is quite clear: it speaks of the *church* in Rome which meets in the home of Priscilla and Aquila (*et domesticam eorum ecclesiam*).

What of Epaenetus? Epaenetus is "beloved"—as is Ampliatus (vs. 8), Stachys (vs. 9), and Persis (vs. 12). We know nothing else, except that Epaenetus was the first convert to Christianity in Asia; but inasmuch as he is mentioned by name, we can assume that he was also instrumental in bringing others to the Christian faith—thus Paul would feel a particularly strong affection for him.

Line 6 brings to notice yet another woman: Mary. She, too, labored for the early Church. The fact that Paul emphasizes the fact that she had "much labored" indicates that she was among the earliest converts to the church in Rome, was a part of its organizing group, and continued her work in the church—probably under the direction of Priscilla (*Salutate Mariam, quae multum laboravit in vobis*) who headed the early group of faithful. Since this is but speculation, should it be fact then might not Priscilla have been a bishop or a co-bishop in the absence of Peter? Every indication is that Paul received most of his information from Priscilla; she would have had to have had power and authority to make such reports; the fact that Paul would cite her and, thus, the reports indirectly shows that her correspondence was certainly not clandestine.

Andronicus and Junias are mentioned in line 7. They were Jewish (cf. 9:3) and "kinsmen" of the Apostle (this need not mean more than that they were Jewish, but could also mean blood relatives, as might be Herodion (vs. 11), Lucius, Jason, and Sosipater (vs. 21) since there are other Jews mentioned who are not called "kinsmen"—or "relatives", as in vs. 3). Andronicus and Junias shared a couple of other distinctions: they had been imprisoned with Paul (although we don't know where), and may have been apostles since they were Christians before Paul's conversion, and were possibly associated with the other apostles in Jerusalem or Judea, for the line reads "who are of importance among the apostles, who were in Christ before I was" (*Salutate Andronicum et Juliam cognatos et concaptivos meos, qui sunt nobiles in apostolis, qui et ante me fuerunt in Christo*).

Verses 8 - 11 are salutations. Urbanus (vs. 9) was probably a native Roman. Aristobulus was not necessarily a Christian—he is mentioned (vs. 10) only because he gave shelter to Christians.[2] At the same time, this verse does not state nor does it imply that all of his household was Christian, any more than it does in the case of Narcissus and his household (vs. 11).

Line 12 has greater importance. It begins with a recognition of two women, Tryphaena and Tryphosa, who were probably sisters. Persis is also mentioned; Persis is also a woman. All three women, the letter acknowledges, "labored in the lord." The fact that Paul refers to Persis as having "labor*ed* much" can only mean that he was not certain if she was still "working" in the missionfield. It does not mean that she was old or infirmed—only that he had no knowledge of her current status and zeal. The fact that Paul calls Persis "the beloved" indicates that she had already earned her recognition among the faithful and in his eyes.

Rufus may be the son of Simon of Cyrene (Mark 15: 21). He too was a "laborer"—as was his mother. His mother is more significant. Although the line literally reads "Salute Rufus chosen in the Lord, and his mother and mine" (*Salutate Rufum electum in Domino, et matrem ejus et meam*), it does not mean that Rufus' mother was also the mother of Paul. Instead, it is to be read and understood that Rufus' mother acted as if she were a mother to him: ministering to his physical and emotional needs—but when or where this mothering took place we have no knowledge.

Line 14 is all-male in nature. It is a statement of a certain community of believers—all of whom are male: "Salute Asyncritus, Phlegon, Hermas, Patrobas, Hermes, and the brethren which are with them." The importance of it is in the location it enjoys; it is after the salutation is played to the prominent women of the community—a salutation usually reserved for men, but in this case, to cite a scripture overly quoted "those who would be first are last, and those who are last become first." The full extent and impact of this reality is seen in the order of the text, lines 12 - 14:

12 Ἀσπάσασθε Τρύφαιναν καὶ Τρυφῶσαι τὰς κοπιώσας ἐν Κυρίῳ. Ἀσπάσασθε Περσίδα τὴν ἀγαπητήν, ἥτις πολλὰ ἐκοπίασεν ἐν Κυρίῳ. 13 Ἀσπάσασθε Ῥοῦφον τὸν ἐκλεκτὸν ἐν Κυρίῳ καὶ τὴν μητέρα αὐτοῦ καὶ ἐμοῦ. 14 Ἀσπάσασθε Ἀσύνκριτον, Φλέγοντα, Ἑρμῆν, Πατρόβαν, Ἑρμᾶν, καὶ τοὺς σὺν αὐτοῖς ἀδελφούς.

The importance of woman returns with line 15. With little doubt, Julia is a woman. It is a common name—one found even among slave women in the imperial household.[3] She may have been the wife of Philogus. That she is coupled with other men and women indicates only that she is a member of the Christian community.

The heart of the letter does not appear until line 16. There the encouragement of the *osculum pacis*, a holy kiss is made—an encouragement which is an enjoinment, and not truly an option. It is similar to Paul's enjoinment to the Christian community at Corinth (I Cor. 16:20; II Cor. 13:12), and to the church at Thessaly (I Thess. 5:26).

15 Ἀσπάσασθε Φιλόλογον καὶ Ἰουλίαν, Νηρέα καὶ τὴν ἀδελφὴν αὐτοῦ, καὶ Ὀλυμπᾶν, καὶ τοὺς σὺν αὐτοῖς πάντας ἁγίους. 16 Ἀσπάσασθε ἀλλήλους ἐν φιλήματι ἁγίῳ. Ἀσπάζονται ὑμᾶς αἱ ἐκκλησίαι πᾶσαι τοῦ Χριστοῦ. 17 Παρακαλῶ δὲ ὑμᾶς, ἀδελφοί, σκοπεῖν τοὺς τὰς διχοστασίας καὶ τὰ σκάνδαλα παρὰ τὴν διδαχὴν ἣν ὑμεῖς ἐμάθετε ποιοῦντας, καὶ ἐκκλίνετε ἀπ' αὐτῶν· 18 Οἱ γὰρ τοιοῦτοι τῷ Κυρίῳ ἡμῶν Χριστῷ οὐ δουλεύουσιν ἀλλὰ τῇ ἑαυτῶν κοιλίᾳ, καὶ διὰ τῆς χρηστολογίας καὶ εὐλογίας ἐξαπατῶσιν τὰς καρδίας τῶν ἀκάκων.

Peter gives the same charge, calling it the kiss of love (I Peter 5:14). It was not a Christian innovation, nor was it sexual in intent or nature. Instead it was a customary greeting which was a token of peace, respect and goodwill: a token Christ demanded from Simon the Pharisee in his reprimand "Do you not give me a kiss?" (Luke 7:45), and which became a sign of hypocrisy when Judas misued it, betraying his Christ (Luke 22:48).

The preeminence and paramount distinction of the church of Rome is testified to when Paul declares that "the churches of Christ salute you" (*Salutant vos omnes ecclesiae Christi*). The significance of this recognition is that the group who receives this letter and this recognition is led by a woman at the time the letter arrives—Phoebe. Peter is not mentioned—therefore he, at least tacitly placed the shepherding of the church into her hands. This is strengthened even further, for Paul immediately gives directions to the community of faithful, expecting Phoebe and the other *ministrae* to see that his word is heard and his injunctions followed:

19 Ἡ γὰρ ὑμῶν ὑπακοὴ εἰς πάντας ἀφίκετο· ἐφ' ὑμῖν οὖν χαίρω, θέλω δὲ ὑμᾶς σοφοὺς εἶναι εἰς τὸ ἀγαθόν, ἀκεραίους δὲ εἰς τὸ κακόν. 20 Ὁ δὲ θεὸς τῆς εἰρήνης συντρίψει τὸν σατανᾶν ὑπὸ τοὺς πόδας ὑμῶν ἐν τάχει. Ἡ χάρις τοῦ Κυρίου ἡμῶν Ἰησοῦ [Χριστοῦ] μεθ' ὑμῶν.

The mood and expression of style is severe. It is an admonition and injunction. It is not a point of reference or a subject for debate. It is a warning, stern and forceful, cautioning the faithful to be aware of false prophets and false teachers. Paul does not include women in either category, nor does he call them heretics or worse. Lines 17-18 considers those who serve their own ends ("their own bellies": *Hujuscemodi enim Christo Domino nostro non serviunt sed suo ventri*) to be "troublemakers" (*seducunt corda innocentium*, literally: "deceive the hearts of the simple"). False teachers could be Judazing zealots, who were Paul's most heated opponents, whom he believed would not only cause divisions within the Christian community, but also narrow its appeal, for few Gentile men relished the prospect of a circumcision. Paul does not want the congregation to take these "false teachers" on—not only because there is a strong possibility that they could not respond to a debate with any learned discourse, but moreso because he believed the holy Spirit would champion the faithful. Throughout his warning there is no mention of the sex of the "deceivers" or the "beguilers". The "innocent" are not defined, either, by gender. The Pauline message is one to all *persons*.

Line 19 reflects once more on the maturity of the church of Rome. The fame of the Christian community at Rome had become universally known, respected, and loved throughout the *corpus Christianorum*. The crucial place Rome and its church played in the scheme of things and in the world as an order, and the church as a whole was major and had to be retained in its purest form. No where does Paul say or imply that the church of Rome in which Phoebe and the other women "labored much" was filled with "false teachings" or any other form of "corruption". He does not ask nor does he demand that Phoebe or any of the other "holy women"—or any of the other women who were not called holy—step down; instead the Apostle reiterates his assurance of their fidelity and rejoices in the good fortune of the church in Rome (vs. 19f). Because of their faith, and the faith of the congregation at Rome,God will crush Satan completely. After this,he gives his benediction, and even allows his secretary,Tertius,to include his own greeting to the church (*Saluto vos ego Tertius, qui scripsi epistulam, in Domino*). The remaining lines are a doxology.

21 Ἀσπάζεται ὑμᾶς Τιμόθεος ὁ συνεργός μου, καὶ Λούκιος καὶ Ἰάσων καὶ Σωσίπατρος οἱ συγγενεῖς μου. 22 Ἀσπάζομαι ὑμᾶς ἐγὼ Τέρτιος ὁ γράψας τὴν ἐπιστολὴν ἐν Κυρίῳ. 23 Ἀσπάζεται ὑμᾶς Γάϊος ὁ ξένος μου καὶ ὅλης τῆς ἐκκλησίας. Ἀσπάζεται ὑμᾶς Ἔραστος ὁ οἰκονόμος τῆς πόλεως καὶ Κούαρτος ὁ ἀδελφός. [24 Ἡ χάρις τοῦ Κυρίου ἡμῶν Ἰησοῦ Χριστοῦ μετὰ πάντων ὑμῶν· ἀμήν.]

So what is the significance of the sixteenth chapter of Paul's letter to the congregation in Rome?

More than anything else Romans 16 shows conclusively that women were co-workers in the early Christian church. Since the letter was written approximately A.D. 57, it demonstrates the extent of the work of women and the high regard they were held in by men of the stature of Paul. The spread of Christianity took place not only because women were accepted into the early church, but because they zealously, devotedly, urgently worked to promote it, spread the gospel, evangelize, and care for those who hungered for some mental relief and promise of a better life to come. Of the twenty-eight people Paul salutes, ten were women—and they came first. Even the highly critical bishop of Constantinople, John Chrysostom, who seldom had little favorable to say about women, had to write concerning Paul's greeting to Mary in Romans 16: 6:[4]

> How is this? A woman is again honored and proclaimed victorious! Again are we men put to shame. Or rather, we are not put to shame only, but have even an honor conferred upon us. For an honor we have, in that there are such women among us, but we are put to shame, in that we men are left so far behind them. . . . For the women of those days were more spirited than lions.

The sixteenth chapter of the Letter to the Romans also gives proof that women were highly literate. Some scholars even believe that Priscilla is the author of the anonymous Letter to the Hebrews in the New Testament. Again, St. John Chrysostom, applauds this possibility indirectly when he writes:[5]

> It is worth examining Paul's motive, when he greets them, for putting Priscilla before her husband. Indeed, he did not say, "Salute Aquila and Priscilla," but rather, "Salute Priscilla and Aquila" [vs. 3] He did not do so without reason: the wife must have

had, I think, greater pity than her husband. This is
not a simple conjecture; its confirmation is evident in
the Acts. Apollos was an eloquent man, well versed
in Scripture, but he knew only the baptism of John;
this woman took him, instructed him in the way of
God, and made of him an accomplished teacher.

The sixteenth chapter of Romans also shows that
at least one woman was numbered among the apostles.
Some rather bad scholars have vainly tried to argue that
Junia is a contraction of a much less common male name,
but John Chrysostom, again, noted, "Oh, how great is the
devotion of this woman that she should be counted
worthy of the appellation of apostle!"[6] —as did Origen of
Alexandria (c. 185-253), Jerome (340/50-419/20), and
other leading thinkers in the early Church.

At the same time, Paul acknowledges that he too, was
subordinate to a woman—a woman who "ruled over" him.
The word he uses is *prostatis*—it means, in all Greek literature, "ruler"—not "helper" as some attempt to feigned argue. The same word appears in the form of a verb
(*proistamenous*) in I Thess. 5:12, and there it is correctly
translated as "rule over," as it is in I Tim. 3:4, 5, and 5:17.
This word and its use is strictly regulated to where the
references are to bishops, priests, and deacons![7]

The Pauline Letter to the Romans, in short, gives us
one of the earliest accounts of the role and significance of
women in the early Christian church and community—
where women served not only as faithful wives, but with
full equality beside men as *ministrae* (priests, bishops, and
deacons) of the faith. To ignore the reality of Romans 16
is to deny the fullness of the Christian life and message.
To refuse to accept women as priests today, is to deny the
historical proof that they were priests in the days of the
apostles who saluted them and were ruled over by them.
At best, the 1983 statement by Pope John Paul II that
"women will never be priests", "because of Scriptural

prohibitions" is ludicrous; at worse the pontifical pronouncement is dangerous, blasphemous, heretical and destructive to the Christian faith, if left unchallenged.

NOTES

[1] Pliny the Younger, *Epitome*, XCVI, in *Pliny: Letters*, with an English translation by William Melmoth (Cambridge, 1958), vol. 2, Bk. X, p. 404.

[2] J.B. Lightfoot, *Saint Paul's Epistle to the Philippians* (London, 1908), pp. 174f.

[3] *Ibid.*, p. 177.

[4] Migne, *Patrologia. . .Graeca*, vol. 51, cols. 668f.

[5] *Ibid.*, cols. 191f.

[6] *The Homilies of St. John Chrysostom, loc. cit..*

[7] J. Massyngberde Ford, "Biblical Material Relevant to the Ordination of Women," in *Journal of Ecumenical Studies* X.4 (Fall, 1973), pp. 676f. See my *Woman in the Apostolic Age* (Mesquite, 1980), and my *History of Ordination of Women in the Early Church* (Saskatoon, 1975).

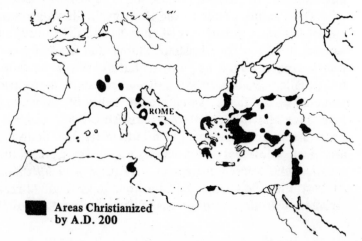

Areas Christianized by A.D. 200

Chapter Seven
Women Ordained to Serve

While the majority of the women who confessed Jesus Christ to be their spiritual lord were followers of their husbands, fathers, older male relatives, and ordained or appointed clergy (*clericos*), some women rose to be leaders of other women and men in the Christian community, both as clergy (*diakonos*), and as governors (*coepiscopoi*). Generally the women who functioned as clergy were called *diakonos*.[1] They enjoyed the same power and responsibilities as men who served Christ. Seldom were these women ever "aids to ministers." A number of the *diakonos*, in fact, commanded the assistance of male clergy; a few even taught the apostles, as did Phoebe who instructed Paul and "ruled over" him.

Those women who chose to "serve the Lord" were ordained in special ceremonies—ceremonies identical to those performed for the ordination of men, and at times performed with the ordination of men.[2] Not only was the ordination of women identical to that of men, but so too, were the responsibilities of the ordained woman equal to that of men.[3]

Their responsibilities could be fulfilled serving a local congregation, or taking up the missionary staff and setting out to bring the "good news" (*gospel*) to those who had not yet heard it. Equal again to men they were called evangelists, and patterned themselves after the celebrated women: Prisca, a certain Mary, Tryphaena, Tryphosa, and Persis, who were known to have "worked hard" (*kopian*) in the service of spreading the Christian faith. The use of the word *kopian* (work) leaves no doubt as to their mission: it is a direct reference to evangelism—a term Paul applied even to himself.[4] Paul wrote that women "labored side by side with me in the gospel together with Clement

and the rest of my fellow workers."[5]   Paul had no difficulty accepting a woman as a "fellow-worker"—a priest, or
deacon—an office firmly established by A.D. 63, when
Paul was quite alive and in the height of his writing career.
He wrote to Timothy (3:8-11): "Deacons also must be serious, not double-tongued, not addicted to much wine, not
greedy for too much bread (literally: "too much grain"),
they must hold the mystery of the faith with a clear con-
science.   And, let them also be tested first; then, if they
prove themselves blameless, let them serve as deacons.   In
the same manner the women deacons (*gynaikas*) must be
serious, not slanderers, but temperate and faithful in all
things."   (Although the word used here to describe women
deacons is *gynaikas*; literally "women"), all early Church
men accepted it as deacons.[6])   The traditionalist who
argue that it is a comment on the wives of deacons overlook the lack of a parallel, as in the case of the wives of
bishops (cf. 3:1-7), and the parallels which exist in every
other instance that referents to husbands and wives occur.
This passage neither states nor was intended to mean the
wives of deacons.   Those traditionalists which cite Paul's
reputed condemnation of women for having caused the
"fall of man" (I Cor. 14:34-35), present an even weaker
case, since the often given line in Corinthians today must
be held suspect, for it is quite widely considered an addition to the original text by later scribes.[7]   Its' addition to
the letter can be explained simply; its there was a
growing hostility in the Roman empire against the Christians, many male Christians assumed that it was at the
instance of powerful Roman women who connived,
consorted, ruled, poisoned, and plotted the overthrow of
the various succeeding impermanent and corrupt
emperors.[8]   Furthermore, many who had an opportunity
to add the offensive line were educated Jewish males well
learned in the antifeminist writings and customs of their
theological and national past and present. Those Christian
apologists and scribes who came out of a Greek back-

ground had a similar conditioning.[9] Not only did Paul *not* condemn women in general, but he had no objections to them being a part of the clergy regular, nor did he oppose them as prophets—quite the contrary, as has been shown earlier in this book, he recognized them as prophets and applauded their "work" as prophets. It would have been considered blasphemy for Paul to reject women as prophets, since Peter himself acknowledged their existence and importance, and on the first Christian Pentecost, declared—quoting Joel 3:15—to the men and women who assembled in the upper room (Acts 1:14; 2:1-4):

> *And in the last days it shall be, God declares,*
> *that I will pour out my Spirit upon* all *flesh,*
> *and your sons and* daughters *shall prophesy,*
> *and your young men shall see visions,*
> *and your old men shall dream dreams;*
> *yes, and on my menservants*
> *and my* maidservants *in those days*
> *I will pour out my Spirit; and they shall prophesy.*

(Acts 2:16-18); and he had met Phillip's four "virgin daughters who were prophets" (Acts 21:7-9) when he came to Caesarea from Ptolemais. The objection of the traditionalist male chauvinists in the Christian clergy is taken out of context, for the passage (I Cor. 11:15) states "For a woman, however, it is a sign of disrespect to her head if she prays or prophesies unveiled". Paul no more damned women for prophesying than for praying—he only admonished women to cover their heads, as do faithful Jewish worshipers. This was undoubtedly stated so that women would not be "set apart" or "recognized on the basis of their sex" within a congregation, for theologically Paul affirmed that "there is neither male nor female" in the eyes of God. Furthermore this passage is an open rejection of the Gnostic affirmation that prayer was to be an act not demonstrative of one's subjection to God but on par with God.

I Corinthians 11:7 is also a delight to the traditionalists. Here it is written that woman is not made in the image of God. Man (*aner*) is glorified; woman is made subject to *aner*. *Anthropos* ("humankind"/"mankind") is not employed. But it, like I Cor. 14:34-35 must be questioned. Lexiographically and syntatically this text is dissimilar to the general Pauline style and vocabulary. It appears to be added, like the rough style found in I Tim. 2:11-12 and 3:11. It is out of line with his remarks in Galatians 3:38, and rapport with women in his other epistles. The same is true of I Cor. 14:34-35 and I Tim. 2:12-15, which are in opposition to Romans 16, and Ephesians 5:25, 28-31 which not only enjoins men to love their wives but also realize that they are "in one flesh" and must therefore act in harmony. If two are as one, neither can be above the other. Sex is not a qualifier for strength or position, since "God is not a respecter of persons" (Acts 10:24). According to the early Apostles, God sees humankind as androgynous.

The Christian androgyny can especially be seen in the term *diakonos*. Paul calls himself the *diakonos* of Jesus Christ.[10] It is the same term used in discussing the role of Stephen and his household: *eis diakonian tois hagiois etaxan heautous*.[11]

In the time of Phoebe *diakonos* is genitive—not dative. *Diakonos* does not indicate the beneficiary of the service, but rather the presenter of the service. She is the minister *of* the church at Cenchreae. Her service, opening in the form of charity to the poor and the giving of the use of her house for religious services was not only the product of the charismatic movement she experienced personally, but was the proper prototype of the office of minister itself.[12] The relationship of this deaconate is seen in Origen's commentary on Paul's letter to the Romans: *feminas in ministeris Ecclesiae constitui* where the Greek would read *kai gynaikas diakonous tes Ekklesias kathistasthai*, in which he declared "This text teaches with the authority of the Apostle that even women are instituted deacons in the Church. . .[and] that women, who have given assistance to so many people and who by their good works deserve to be praised by the Apostle, ought to be accepted in the diaconate [*in minsterium* (Latin) / *eis diakonian* (Greek)]".

Women were ordained. The eighth book of the *Apostolic Constitutions* states clearly, in its rite of ordination, that women, too, were ordained:

Eternal God, Father of our Lord Jesus Christ, Creator of man and woman, who filled Mary, Deborah, Anna, and Hulda with the Spirit, Who let Your Only Son be born of a woman, who instituted women-guardians for the holy gates of the Tent of Witness and of the Temple: look now upon this Your servant who has been elected for Your ministry; give her the Holy Spirit and purify her from all sin of the body and soul that she may worthily fulfill the function assigned to her, to Your glory, and to the praise of Your Christ—with Whom be to You the glory and worship, and to the Holy Spirit for ever. Amen.(Let it be so)

Ἐπίκληις ἐπι χειροτονιας δια-κονισσης. Ὁ Θεὸς ὁ αιωνιος ὁ Πατὴρ τοῦ Κυπίου ημῶν Ιησοῦ Χριστοῦ, ὁ ἀνδρὸς χυὶ γυναιχὸς δημιουργὸς · ὁ πληρώσος Πνεύματος Μαριὰμ χαι Δεβόῤῥαν· χαι Ἄνναν χαι Ὁλδὰν ὁ μή ἁπαξιωσος τὸν μονογενῆ σου μαρτυρίπν χαι ἐν ναῷ προχειρισάμενος τὰς φρουροὺς τῶν ἁγιων σου πυλῶν αὐτῇ Πνεῦμα ἅγιον, χαι χαθάρισον αὐτὴν ἀπὸ παντὸς μολυσμοῦ σαρχὸς χαι πνεύματος πρὸς τὸ ἐπαξίως ἐπιτελειν αὐτὴν τὸ ἐγχειρισθὲν αυτη αὐτῇ ἔργον εἰς δόξαν σὴν χαι προσχύνηοις χαὶ τῶ ἁγίω Πνεύματι εἰς τοὺς αἰῶνες. Ἀμην

As late as the fourth century the Syrian (and some other eastern bishops) followed the Apostolic Constitutions which *ordered* them to ordain women: *"Ordain (procheir-isia) also a woman deacon (diakonon) who is faithful and holy".*[13] In many instances they followed the following prayer-ritual:[14]

*Concerning a deaconess (*diakonissa*), I Bartholomew
make this constitution: O Bishop, thou shalt lay thy hands
upon her (*epitheseis aute tas cheiras*) in the presence of the
presbytery, and of the deacons and deaconesses, and shalt
say:* O Eternal God, the Father of our Lord Jesus Christ,
the Creator of man and woman, who didst replenish with
the Spirit Miriam, and Deborah, and Anna, and Huldah;
who didst not disdain that Thy only begotten Son should
be born of a woman; who also in the tabernacle of the
testimony, and in the temple didst ordain women to be
keepers of Thy holy gates, do Thou now also look down
upon this Thy servant, who is to be ordained (*procheir-
izomenen*) to the office of a woman deacon (*diakonian*),
and grant her Thy Holy Spirit, and "cleanse her from all
filthiness of flesh and spirit," that she may worthily dis-
charge the work which is committed to her to Thy glory,
and the praise of Thy Christ, with whom glory and adora-
tion be to Thee and the Holy Spirit for ever. Amen.

Hippolytus (c. A.D. 170 - 235) accords it as being
from the Apostles.[15] and the early Councils of the Church
did the same: ratifying it both at Nicaea and Chalcedon.
The Council of Nicaea referred to the women deacons as
clerics:[16]

Likewise, however, both deaconesses (*diakonisson*)
and in general all those who are numbered among the
clergy [*kanoni* (Greek) / *clericos* (Latin): the retain the
same form, authority, and meaning] should retain the
same form.

The Council of Chalcedon (A.D. 451) ruled on the
actual ordination of women, her ministry, and her
liturgy:[17]

A woman should not be ordained (*cheirotonesthai*
[Greek] / *ordinandam* [Latin]) a deaconess before she is
forty. And if after receiving ordination (*cheirothesian*)

she continued in her ministry (*leitourgia*) . . .[she shall follow the same guidelines as a man similarly ordained].

Why the western Roman Catholic Church (or any Christian church) should now question the *right* of women to receiving holy orders as priest and bishop is hard to understand; at best it is ignorance of history of the Church and the writings of the Fathers, and at worse it is an open defiance of God's will and blatant sexism that will lead to the destruction and erasure of the true *corpus Christianorum*, for even Tertullian recognized women *in ecclesiasticis ordinibus*.[18]

The deaconesses of the early Church were more than "aids" to the male clergy. Instead they functioned as equals. They taught and ministered. as recorded in the *Didascalia* (III.12): *And when she is being baptized has come up from the water, let the deaconess receive her, and* teach and instruct *her how the seal of baptism ought to be kept unbroken in purity and holiness. For this cause we say that the* ministry of a woman deacon *is especially needful and important. For our Lord and Savior also was ministered unto by* women ministers. . . .*And thou also hast need of the* ministry of a deaconess *for many things*.[19] The similarity, the identical nature, of the duties of a male and a female cleric was spelled out in the early Church documents; for the word χειροτονιας : (or) *chierotonia* is used both for the man and the woman.[20]

The argument that the duties of the *deaconess* was to be exclusive to and for other women (an argument, I sadly lament, I had even entertained in an earlier edition of this work, before I had completed further research which has made this edition a necessity) is not born out by the records of the day. The deaconess *did* administer to women on behalf of the bishop, but also to men. In part the need for women to administer and minister to women was because of the blatant sexism in the male clergy. Many male clergy feared "contamination" if they came too close or in contact with women.[21] Thus some demanded they (women) be veiled;[22] while others urged that they be excluded 'from all male company."[23] The lessening of the role and responsibilities of women clergy came when they were allowed to "perform their function" only in the absence of the male bishop—or if the number of baptisms grew to such a point that the bishop was unable to perform all at any time—or that baptisms were needed in more places than the bishop could go to and still keep up with the diocesean work required. The same was also true in the early days of the Christian church in the area of the other sacraments, such as penance, confirmation, marriage, and the rest. Initially the women ministers (or *deaconesses*) assisted or performed these rites or sacraments. It would not be for hundreds of years that these responsibilities and privileges would be forbidden women clergy.[24]

The removal of rights and responsibilities from women clergy came only because of the sexual threat women clergy posed to male clergy. Women clergy were popular, being more empathetic and sympathetic to the needs of a congregation—frequently finding the fine shades of grey in any theology that can comfort and aid in the spiritual growth of those who could not or would not accept the rigid ossification of the developing canons of the Church. Male clergy were more staid, demanding a clear and closed canon of rules—as if God had become silent, feeling that revelation was complete and all that need be known was in the canons of Scripture and the Fathers—unless modified, changed, or added and/or deleted by seasoned, old, and angry men who saw their own world (which had been created by God) as a "den of evil" and all who "live within are evil" and thus needed strict guidelines and unchangable rules to "secure salvation." As the political and social situation within the Roman Empire deteriorated, many men and women who were numbered in the congregation of Christians in despair and desperation cried out for a rigid canon, as change became too regular and too chaotic. A single ruler with a single law in a single world was sought: a *tyrannos* (Greek: "absolute ruler"). This "sovereign" would become the emperor in the East, and the Pope in the West. While the *tyrannos* remained within the secular world in the East, the office of deaconess remained in existence and popular.[25] The popularity of deaconesses in the East did not decline until the rule of Julian the Apostate, who in his efforts to resurrect the Old Rome, bringing back the pagan gods and their priestesses, encouraged Christian deaconesses to join "the old faith" and renounce their vows of celibacy and obedience to the bishops. Some women did—and their apostacy was not forgotten by their colleagues or their congregations. Some congregations even went back to the old faiths of ancient Rome, following in the footsteps of their ministers who became priestesses to the old deities. This led many male clergy into ruling against the order of deaconesses and women ministers. In their zeal to preserve the purity of the office of deacon and the Christian faith, these "guardians" ruled against the ministry of *all* women. But this "stamping out of women clergy" took centuries, for women remained members of the clergy as late as the sixth century, when the most celebrated deaconess of the orient, the famed Greek Olympias, was ordained by Bishop Nebridios. She became a loyal and lasting friend of St. John Chrysostom. There is an apocryphal account of her acceptance by the Golden Tongued Orator (St. John Chrysostom), which runs, that when she was questioned concerning her duties "which belong fitly to a man," Olympia responded by inquirying, "When the flock are hungry and there is no shepherd, are the sheep to starve, and haven't women been shepherdess since time began? Is the faith of Christ so weak that it can be administered only by a man?"[26]

Other women chose a life ministering to the physical needs of the faithful. In Asia Minor the majority of deaconesses worked in hospitals. In the Mid-East they served in colonies set aside for the terminally or critically ill, as well as cared for the elderly and the very young. These were the earliest orders of sisters or nuns, many which retained their episcopal dignity and control, as will be discussed later. There was little question and no problem with the order of women in the Church for the civil authorities. The emperor Justinian placed the order of deaconess among the clergy in all civil records as late as 16 March 535.[27] The churches in the East accepted them and their authority as late as the twelfth century.[28]

The order of deaconess was still alive in the West in the fourth century. Nectaria was the last woman raised to the office and dignity of deaconess in the west. She was ordained by Elpidius, bishop of Satala—an action which cost him his episcopal appointment, for he was deposed by the Council of Constantinople which feared that the increasing number of women who sought out holy orders would discourage men from a similar quest.[29] This gynophobia was continued in A.D. 380, at the I Council of Saragossa,[30] and the Council of Nimes (A.D. 394/6).[31] In both cases the canons which ruled against women being in the clergy gave an understatement on the gynophobia that was growing in the psychology of men. This became increasingly more public in following councils: Canon 26 of the Council of Orange (A.D. 441), declared "Let no one proceed to the ordination of deaconesses *anymore.*"; canon 21, of the A.D. 517 Council of Epaon, defining "We abrogate completely in the entire kingdom the consecration of widows who *are* named deaconesses." and the II Council of Orleans (A.D. 533) which spat "*No longer* shall the blessing of *women deaconesses* be given, because of the weakness of the sex." In every case, in addition to ruling against women in the role and authority of deaconess, the councils openly acknowledged the existence of women who functioned as ministers at the time of their denunciation. In light of these statements, and others,[32] it is illiterate and immature to declare that women did not serve as priests and clergy in the early Church.[33]

Women as Priests

Were women ever called *priests*? The answer is yes! To present this argument we must turn to the Greek, as the English word "priest" is derived from the Greek word *presbyteros*. The women who served the church at Ephesus were called *presbyteros*, as were the women which were discussed by the writer of the deutero-Pauline First Epistle to Timothy (5:1-2: *Do not rebuke a male presbyter (*presbytero*) but exhort him as you would a father; treat younger men like brethren, women presbyters (*presbyteras*) like mothers, younger women like sisters.)* The author notes that Timothy was "ordained" by the elderhood (or presbyterate: *presbyteriou* in 4:14), before he discusses the presbyters which he is to be in charge of and over (he is called *episkopos* in 3:1). This is a collegiate sentence: he is the bishop and they are priests who are learning to become "as he."

The unique distinction between "priest"/"priestess" and "deacon"/"deaconess" did not become defined until the pontificate of Gelasius (A.D. 492-496), who ruled that the priest/ess "ministered the faith" directly from Christ, while the deacon/ess ministered the faith for and through Christ. This distinction raised the priest/ess slightly higher than the deacon/ess.[34]

Most of the early priestesses served the *paganus*—or country-folk, preparing the way for later evangelists, such as Sts. Cyril and Methodius. Their tasks were sacerdotal and sacramental in nature, serving at the suffrance of the metropolitan see but on the fringe of the orthodox community. Among these "country priests" was Firmilian of Caesarea in Cappadocia. Highly educated, literate in languages, and zealous for the Christian faith, Firmilian wrote to Bishop Cyprian of Carthage in the middle of the third century, detailing the needs and accomplishments of her ministry and the development of the Christian church in her area.[35] Cyprian had only praise for Firmilian. There is no condemnation of her tasks, her rank or her authority as priest. Condemnations of women as priests and spokespersons for Christ will be condemned only in general terms, and then only when it seemed certain that the condemnations would not reach the ears or eyes of those women who "fight valiantly for the faith, bringing new souls daily to Christ"

Women as Bishop

Women were not only priests, but also bishops in the early Catholic Church. They have served as bishops since the first days of the Christian community.

St. John, known as "the Beloved" was among the first apostles to recognize women and their role as bishops in the early community: addressing his second letter to the *eklekta* ("Elect Lady") of the Church. He begins his letter with a salutation: *"The bishop to the elect Lady and her children, whom I love in the truth—and not only I but also they that have known the truth—for the truth's sake, which dwells in us, and shall be with us for ever: Grace be with you, mercy and peace, from God the Father, and from the Lord Jesus Christ, the Son of the Father, in truth and love."* (The Latin reads: *Senior electa dominae et natis ejus, quos ego diligo in veritate, et non ego solus sed et omnes qui cognoverunt veritatem, propter veritatem quae permanet in nobis et nobiscus erit in aeternum. Sit nobiscum gratia misericordia, pax a Deo Patre et Christo Jesu Filio Patris in veritate et caritate.*) The importance of this address is immeasurable and of the greatest significance. John is the Πρεσβυτεροσ or "elder": the bishop/*presbyteros*, and he salutes the "elect Lady": elect in this case, as in American political terminology for a future president who is styled the "president-elect", is a reference to her soon-to-be-realized elevation within the

Christian community and Church's hierarchy. Her children (*natis ejus*) are the congregation who are seen as
children before God who is the Father (*Deo Patria*). The
magnitude of her authority is seen in the coupling of the
words *eklekte kyria* (or εκλεκτη κυρια in the Greek), for
kyria (κυρια) is parallel to "Lord" (or *kyrios*), and thus has
the function of an "overseer" which can be determined
from the continuance of the salutation which recognizes
her children which may be interpreted either as the
churches under her dominion and/or the "children" (congregation) of the church. An argument for the "children"
being the congregation is best taken from the last line,
where again the *elect* nature of the "Lady" is noted and
hallmarked with the writer's desire to speak with *her*
"*face to face*" than by letter ("*I would rather not use
paper and ink. . . "*.). The rest of the introduction reads:

Ὁ ΠΡΕΣΒΥΤΕΡΟΣ ἐκλεκτῇ κυρίᾳ

καὶ τοῖς τέκνοις αὐτῆς, οὓς ἐγὼ

ἀγαπῶ ἐν ἀληθείᾳ, καὶ οὐκ ἐγὼ μόνος

ἀλλὰ καὶ πάντες οἱ ἐγνωκότες τὴν

ἀλήθειαν, 2 Διὰ τὴν ἀλήθειαν τὴν μέ-

νουσαν ἐν ἡμῖν, καὶ μεθ' ἡμῶν ἔσται

εἰς τὸν αἰῶνα. 3 Ἔσται μεθ' ἡμῶν

χάρις, ἔλεος, εἰρήνη παρὰ θεοῦ πατρὸς

καὶ παρὰ [Κυρίου] Ἰησοῦ Χριστοῦ τοῦ

υἱοῦ τοῦ πατρός, ἐν ἀληθείᾳ καὶ ἀγάπῃ.

4 Ἐχάρην λίαν ὅτι εὕρηκα ἐκ τῶν

τέκνων σου περιπατοῦντας ἐν ἀληθείᾳ

καθὼς ἐντολὴν ἐλάβομεν παρὰ τοῦ

πατρός.

with the Syriac reading as:

ܩܫܝܫܐ ܠܓܒܝܬܐ ܡܪܬܐ
ܘܠܒܢܝܗ . ܐܝܠܝܢ ܕܐܢܐ ܪܚܡ
ܐܢܐ ܒܫܪܪܐ ܃ ܠܐ ܗܘܐ ܕܝܠܝ ܐܢܐ
ܒܠܚܘܕ ܃ ܐܠܐ ܟܠܗܘܢ ܐܝܠܝܢ
ܕܝܕܥܝܢ ܠܫܪܪܐ . 2 ܡܛܠ ܫܪܪܐ
ܗܢܐ ܕܡܩܘܐ ܒܢ . ܘܥܡܢ ܐܝܬܘܗܝ
ܠܥܠܡ . 3 ܬܗܘܐ ܥܡܟܘܢ ܛܝܒܘܬܐ
ܘܪܚܡܐ ܘܫܠܡܐ ܡܢ ܐܠܗܐ ܐܒܐ .
ܘܡܢ ܡܪܢ ܝܫܘܥ ܡܫܝܚܐ ܒܪܗ
ܕܐܒܐ ܃ ܒܫܪܪܐ ܘܒܚܘܒܐ . 4 ܚܕܝܬ
ܛܒ ܃ ܕܐܫܟܚܬ ܡܢ ܒܢܝܟܝ
ܕܡܗܠܟܝܢ ܒܫܪܪܐ ܃ ܐܝܟ ܦܘܩܕܢܐ
ܕܢܣܒܢ ܡܢ ܐܒܐ .

The second line of this letter is a statement of belief that Christianity has a monopoly on truth–and that this truth will always stay with Christians. It, too, is a mark of distinction for it sets the Christian community apart from all other societies which, indirectly, do not have "the truth"–the fact that John accords the Elect Lady the dominion over this truth by having charge of the children which "have also known the truth" again marks her as a special person–not one of the congregation, nor even one of the general *ministers* of the congregation–instead it suggests that she is over the children which are her children.

Although the third sentence in this Second Letter of

John is a standard greeting on a first reading, a second reading shows that the Elect Lady is singled out for a special dispensation of God's love, mercy, and grace—which, undoubtedly is the reason why the writer of the letter found her children (v. 4) "walking in the truth".

That the Elect Lady has been given charge over determining who "enters" her house is seen in lines 7-10, for the writer declares *"If anyone comes to you and does not bring this doctrine, do not receive him into the house"*. This line can be interpreted in two ways: the initial interpretation being that the Elect Lady is not to receive anyone who is not "orthodox" in their belief (holding the established Christian faith) must not be allowed to enter her home; however, in line with Romans 16, where the house was almost always the meeting place of the early Christians, it should be interpreted as "church" which would then render the line to state that the Elect Lady (or bishop-elect) was not to admit into the Church any person (regardless of gender) into communion who did not adhere to the established interpretation of the Christian faith. That the latter interpretation is the best (and the correct) interpretation can be seen from the impact of the sentence structure and its organization. The sentence is an injunction: *do not* is emphatic. She is to follow the order of the Apostles since she has become "elect" to their number. That she had the episcopal power to contain, control, and commission the work of the Church can again be seen in the word "Elect": as Clement of Alexandria wrote about "elect persons"—a designation for officers of the Church: *"there are many other precepts written in the sacred books which pertain to elect persons (*prosopa eklekta*): certain of these are for priests (*presbyterios*), others indeed for bishops (*episkopois*) others for deacons, still other for widows (*kerais).*[3][6] . ."

The author of I Timothy also acknowledges the existence of women in the early Church. With precise detail the writer instructs bishops on how they are to act—there is no genderal reference, for bishops, only for deaconesses (as discussed earlier). [37]

Women continued to serve as bishops after the time of the apostles. In Western Europe, female bishops are found to administer dioceses as late as the fifth century. [38] Female bishops governed churches much later in Ireland. [39] And the abbesses of Las Huelgas of Burgos ruled exempt from male episcopal control for nearly seven hundred years (1188-1874), enjoying the right and power to examine apostolic notaries (as well as royal and even imperial notaries), unite parishes, transfer benefices, rebuild churches, hear matrimonial cases, hear and judge criminal cases, approve confessors from among both the regular and the secular clergy, impose interdict and censure, and even to license bishops to exercise pontifical rites within her diocese: *nullis diocesis.* [40]

NOTES

[1] Roger Gryson, *Le Ministère des femmes dans l'Eglise ancienne* (Gembloux, Belgium, 1972), chap. 1; an English edition, appearing under the title *Women in the Ministry of the Early Church*, trans. by Jean LaPorte and Mary Louise Hall has been published by the Liturgical Press (Collegeville, MN: 1976), see pp. 87f.

[2] *Ibid.*, pp. 138f.

[3] Apostolic Constitutions III.16.1, in Alexander Roberts and James Donaldson (eds.), *The Ante-Nicene Fathers*, (Grand Rapids, MI: Wm. B. Erdmanns, 1951), vol. 7, p. 431; cf. Jean Danielou, *The Ministry of Women in the Early Church* (London: Meuthen, 1961), pp. 22ff.

[4] Cf. Phil. 4:2-3; Rom. 16; II. Tim. 4:19, 21; cp. Migne, *Patrologica Graeca*, vol. 51, cols. 668f.

[5] Phil. 4:2-3.

[6] Gryson, *loc. cit.*

[7]G. Fitzer, "Das Weib Schweige in der Gemeinde," in *Uber den unaulinischen Charakter der Muliertacet-Verse in I Korinther 14* (Munich, 1963). The same is true for I Tim. 2:11-12, and 3:11; cf. C. Spicq, *Saint Paul, Les Epitres pastorales* (Paris, 1969), p. 456. Cp. my *Woman and St. Paul: A Study of the Pauline Letters on Woman and Woman's Role in the Christian Church* (Cincinnati, 1968).

[8]James Donaldson, *Woman: Her Position and Influence in Ancient Greece and Rome, and among the Early Christians* (London, 1907), pp. 77-147; R. Schilling, "Vestales et vierges chretiennes dans la Rome antique," in *Revue des Sciences Religieuses* 35 (1961) pp. 113-129; and my *Woman in ancient Rome, loc. cit.*

[9]A major debate exists on the nature of Paul and his heritage. James Cleugh, in *Love Locked Out* (London, 1963), p. 12, argues that Paul was "a bald, bandy-legged, and beetle-browed renegade Jew," whose negative attitude towards women and sex is due to his rejection as a suitor, to Joseph A. Grassi, author of "Women's Liberation: The New Testament Perspective," in *The Living Light: A Christian Educational Review*, 8, no. 2 (Summer, 1971), p. 29, states that "Paul frequently acknowledged the work of women as active collaborators in the apostolate as well as assistants in good works"; there is more foundation for the latter argument, as I elaborate on in my *Woman and St. Paul*, with references and discussions on the "negative aspects" of Paul's writings which appear to be "anti-woman," which are, for the most part, suspect by most scholars who feel, as I do, that they were later additions. If the passages in question are truly Pauline, it would be better to interpret them as opposed to what women represent *sexually* rather than an opposition to the sex (or gender) of womanhood. Paul appears to be more concerned with the issue of human sexuality, idolatry, money, and personal freedom than with gender; see Charles Seltman, *Women in Antiquity* (London, 1956), pp. 184-188.

[10]Rom. 11:13; I Cor. 3:5; II Cor. 3:4-6:13.

[11]I Cor. 16:15.

[12]A. Oepke, "Gyne," in *TDNT*, I (English ed.), p. 787.

[13]III.6, 1. in Roberts and Donaldson, *loc. cit.*

[14]*Ibid.*, p. 492.

[15]My *Woman in early Christianity and Christian Society*, p. 11 citing canon 19.

94

[16]J. D. Mansi, *Sacrorum conciliorum nova et amplissa collectio* (Florence, 1757-1798), vol. 2, pp. 676ff.

[17]*Ibid.*, vol. 7, p. 364.

[18]Migne, *Patrologia Latina*, vol. 2, col. 978.

[19]This was authored in the early third-century A.D.

[20]Migne, *Patrologia Graeca*, vol. 8, col. 31, 2.

[21]See Origen, *Selecta in Exodus* XVIII.17, in Migne, *ibid.*, vol. 12, cols. 296f; Epiphanius, *Adversus Collyridianos*, in Migne, *ibid.*, vol. 42, cols. 740ff.; John Chrysostom, "Letter to Theodora," chap. 14, in *Sources chretiennes*, vol. 117, p. 167; all in the East; in the West, the attitude is expressed by Augustine of Hippo, who, after having a mistress for some time, and having a son by the mistress, rallied against women, declaring "I feel that nothing so casts down the manly mind from its height as the fondling of a woman and those bodily contacts which belong to the married state" in his *Soliloquies* 1.10, and in his *De Trinitate* (7.7, 10), argues that a woman is not created in the image of God; who was joined by Pope Gregory "the Great" (A.D. 540-604), who arqued that woman was the essence of weakness, and the destruction of man; see Migne, *Patrologia Latina*, vol. 75, cols. 982f. Galen expressed the same opinion in his medical treatise *De Uteri Dissectione*, for which he was accepted by the Christian church and its ministry to the physical care and cure of its faithful; cp. Jerome, Epistle 48:14 *"If it is good not to touch a woman, then it is bad to touch a woman always and in every case."*, Migne, *Patrologia Latina*, vol. 30, col. 732.

[22]Cf. I Cor. 11:3, 7-9; Jerome, Epistle, 22.7.

[23]Dionysius of Alexandria, Canonical Epistle, chap. 2, in Migne, *Patrologia Graeca*, vol. 10, col. 1282; cp. Tertullian, *De culte feminarum*; and Ambrosiaster, in Migne, *Patrologia Latina*, vol. 17, cols. 253ff.

[24]Cyprian, *Epistle* 74 (75) 10, 11 in *Corpus scriptorum ecclesiasticorum latinorum* (Vienna), vol. 3, pp. 817f. The current twentieth century attempt by the Roman Catholic Church, and especially by Pope John Paul II to suppress the right of women to be ordained priests, is best seen in *Declaration on the Question of the Admission of Women to the Ministerial Priesthood*, in *Acta Apostolica Sedis* 69 (29 Februarii 1977) pp. 98-116. The majority of the arguments against the ordination of women—like the nonsense pronouncements by John Paul II—are based on spurious psuedocanons ranging from the *Statuta Ecclesiae Antique* (reputedly written at IV Council of

Carthage in A.D. 398, or at the turbulent Synod of Valentia in Gaul in A.D. 347, but most likely penned in the city of Arles around A.D. 525), and the Psuedo-Isodorian Decretals—one of the most famous and best known forgeries in history, written probably at Rheims (or, LeMans?) around 845-852. Cf. A.G. Cicognani, *Canon Law*, 2d rev. ed. (Philadelphia, 1935), pp. 222, 243.

[25]Cyprian, *loc. cit.* Sozonmen, *Ecclesia Historia* 4:24, 16.

[26]Migne, *Patrologia Graeca*, vol. 47, cols. 56a-58a, 60a-61d. On her friendship with John Chrysostom, see, *ibid.*, col. 35bc. On the work of other deaconesses, see J. Germer-Durand, "Epigraphie chretienne de Jerusalem," in *Revue Biblique* I (1892) pp. 560-588, no. 10, and *Monumenta Asia Minoris, Antiqua*, vol. 1, ed. W.M. Calder (London, 1928), nos. 323b, 324, 326, 383, 178, 194, and 226. Also see *Corpus inscriptionom latinarum* 3:13845, and 5:6467 for references. Women still functioned in Orleans as late as A.D. 533 as acknowledged at the II Council of Orleans which repeated its ban on the ordination of women—a ban many bishops continued to ignore; see Canon 21 in *Corpus Christianorum Latinorum*, as for particulars in 148A, 29, 163-165.

[27]*Ibid.*

[28]See my *Woman in the Twelfth Century* (Denison, 1972).

[29]Sozonmen, *loc. cit.*

[30]Canon 1.

[31]*Corpus Christianorum Latinorum 148:50, 14-19.*

[32]Clothar I acknowledged their existence "and valued ministry" (see *Monumenta Germaniae Historica*, AA. 4-2, 41, 20-31), cp. *Corpus Christianorum Latinorum* 148A, 187, 341ff.

[33]It is refreshing to read the enlightend and educated comments of Leonard and Arlene Swidler, in their work *Women Priests: A Catholic Commentary on the Vatican Declaration* (Ramsey, NJ, 1977), and the superb article "Junia. . . Outstanding Among the Apostles" by Bernadette Brooten, in Swidler and Swidler, *ibid.*, pp. 141ff. which gives a totally convincing scholarly analysis not only to the fact that Junia *was* an apostle, but why women must be allowed to resume their role as priests in the Catholic Church. One can only feel pity for John Paul II and his poor showing as a spokesperson for Christ when he declared that women would "never" be priests—an office women have every legal, historical, and theological

right to hold, occupy, and speak from.

[34] His *Epistle* 26.

[35] *Corpus scriptorum ecclesiasticorum latinorum* 3:817-818.

[36] Migne, *Patrologia Graeca*, vol. 8, col. 675.

[37] See pages 40-47. Also see my *Woman in the Apostolic Age*.

[38] Council of Tours, canon 20. F. Gross-Gondi, *Trattato di Epigrafia Christiana* (Roma, 1920), p. 153; G. Marini, *Inscriptiones Christianes*, MS Vatica 9072, pt. ii, chap. xxii, no. 1, 1608.

[39] Cogitosus, "Vita Sanctae Brigidae," in Thomas Messingham, *Florilegum Insulae Sanctorum seu Vitae et Acta Sanctorum Hiberniae* (Paris, 1624), chap. 4, pp. 193ff.

[40] Domenico Morea and Francisco Muciaccia, *Le Pergamme di Conversano* (Trani, 1943), XXVII, perg. 5, p. 7 gives an Italian account, while the Spanish is given by Francesco de Berganza, *Antiguedades de España* (Francesco del Hierro, 1721), Pt. 2, Lib. 4, chap. 6. Cp. Archives of the abbey, *Leg.* 7, 261 ARM. German abbesses had a similar power, especially at St. Mary's Uberwasser, where the abbess represented the local bishop in all church and civil affairs. See F. E. Kettner, *Antiquitates Quedlinburgenses* (Leipzig, 1712), pp. 39-42; and, Edmund E. Stengel, "Die Grabschrift der ersten abtissim von Quedliburg," in *Deutsche Archives für Geschichte des Mittelalter* (Weimar, 1939), pp. 164ff; with the most interesting discussion in Rudolf Schulze, *Das adelige Frauen— (Kanonissen)—Slift der Hl. Maria und Die Pfarre Liebfrauen-Uberwasser za Munster* (Munster, 1962), pp. 23-27. Some English abbesses enjoyed similar power, with the Synod of Hertford (canon 3) granting immunity from a local bishop's interference on abbey matters (see Dorothy Whitelock (ed.), *English Historical Documents* vol. 1 (London, 1955), p. 651. See also my *Special Sisters: Woman in the European Middle Ages* (Mesquite, 1983), and my *Woman in the European Middle Ages* (Dallas, 1979). With the Synod of Nidd English abbesses were invited to attend church councils in England; see A. W. Haddon & William P. Stubbs, *Councils and Ecclesiastical Documents Relating to Great Britain and Ireland* (Oxford, 1871), vol. 3, p. 264; and, Whitelock, *op. cit.*, p. 695. Compare their power with that enjoyed by the female ministers and bishops in the first century; see L. Zscharnack, *Der Dienst der Frau in den ersten Jahrhunderten der christlichen Kirche* (Gottingen, 1902), pp. 103-104.

Chapter Eight
St. Paul's Views on Women in the Priesthood

Woman's daily life in the early Christian community, in the Apostolic Age, was directly affected by the teaching and writings of Saul of Tarsus who converted to Christianity after he fell from his horse. The fall itself has been widely discussed; in select writings it has been argued that Saul's fall from an earthly mount was tantamount to Adam's fall from grace in Gan Eden—however, that this fall of Saul's was commissioned and in fact forced by the hand and will of God, and thus undid the fall of Adam, returning humankind to a special grace. The mind of God however is too great for this author to speculate upon or hypothesize about, all that can be said at this time is that Saul's attitude towards women changed immediately after his fall. Prior to the fall Saul was definitely anti-woman. After the fall Saul, who became known as Paul, was at least neutral towards woman if not, in fact as I argue in my book *Paul and Women*, pro-woman.

There is no biography of Paul. There are many sketches of his life as can be gleaned from the New Testament. But none of these sketches are filled in with the necessary pigments of fact to flush out the full color of this determiner and director of the evolution of Christianity.

Only two things can definitely be said about Saul of Tarsus, or St. Paul the Apostle: one, that he was born an orthodox Jew; and, two, that he was a radical. His Jewish heritage made him neutral to anti-woman, and can be an explanation for the often quoted passages demanding that women be silent in churches, and to wear veils in churches—if those passages are indeed his, which I sincerely doubt—since both the silence of women in the synagogue and the covering of women's bodies was an integral part of Jewish society and thus his own background and psychology. At the same time he was a radical: demanding women stay single if they were widows or unmarried—which was in direct opposition to the custom and expectations of the society of his day which scorned the single individual as one denying her/his obligation to YHWH to "go forth, be fruitful and multiply." (I Cor. 7:8-9). At the same time Paul did not shun the company of women, but in fact was not only to be found among and around women, but saluted those women who "worked for the faith" "as I do". Thus he greets Apphia as "our sister", who together with Philemon and Acrchippus was a leader of the church in Colossae (Philemon 2), as was also the case with the wealthy businesswoman Lydia who hailed from Thyatira (Acts 16:14), Nympha of Laodicea (Col. 4:15), Prisca and Aquila in Rome (Romans 16:3-5, 19), and Chloe in Corinth (I Cor. 1:11)

At the same time Paul enjoins women to "work with him", and makes them co-workers" as with Prisca; "ministers (*diakonos*)" as with Phoebe; or "joint apostles" as with Junia (cf. Romans 16:6, 12; I Thess. 5:12; I Cor. 16:16ff)—with some doing battle for the Lord in stride with him, as did Euodia and Syntyche (Philippians 4:2f).

Paul did not believe that women were to be, *en toto*, subject or subordinate to him. Prisca was certainly independent of Paul, and was never subject to his authority.[1] He not only salutes the lady Prisca, but admonishes the church of Rome to obey her, and tells the Gentiles to be grateful for the missionary work and zeal of Prisca and her husband Aquila—who was secondary if not subordinate to his wife, as can be seen in the fact that when Paul does mention them he always puts Prisca first—a noteworthy point inasmuch as men traditionally were numbered first when women were discussed. In part this could be a public recognition of Prisca's great zeal and success as a missionary, especially after she was able to convert Apollos in Ephesus (Acts 18:18, 26; cf. Romans 16:3f, Corinthians 16:19; II Timothy 4:19).[2]

Not only did Paul acknowledge women to be co-workers, but joint apostles, as was the case with Junia (Romans 16:7). She was a missionary who had been converted to Christianity before Paul fell from his horse. They probably met Paul in the same prison where they were applauded as fellow prisoners "outstanding among the apostles" (Romans 16:7). Junia was not alone in this distinction.[3]

That Paul considered the work of women to be equal to his own, and that he accepted women on par with himself and other men can be seen in his using the term *diakonos* together with *synergos*: minister *and* co-worker (I Cor. 3:5, 9, and, II Cor. 6:1, 4). These *diakonia* were not just occasional or itinerant ministers, but leaders of churches, authorities in the early Christian communities, teachers, and spokespersons (or bishops) in the Apostolic Age (I Thess. 5:12; I Tim. 3:4f, and 5:17; Romans 16, I Cor. 3:5, 9).[4]

Additional insight into the psychology of Paul and his attitude towards women can be seen in the *Acts of Paul and Thelca*, a second-century writing which is entirely devoted to the story of a woman missionary. Thelca, being converted by Paul, takes a vow of continence and is persecuted by her fiance and family who bring her to trial for going against the wishes of the father and the expectations of society. She is condemned to death, but through a miracle is saved, and goes with Paul to Antioch. She is pursued by a Syrian who falls in love with her, and when she rejects his advances, takes his revenge by turning her over to the authorities who condemn her to fight wild beasts. After baptizing herself the beasts leave her alone, and she is set free. She converts Tryphena, her protectoress, and her protectoress' household, and then joins Paul on his journey to Myra where she is commissioned to "teach the word of God". This gives additional impact to women to serve God as missionaries, and many third century women cite this when claiming their right to teach and baptize.[5]

The story of Paul and Thelca is apocryphal. Still it has merit. The story of Paul and Thelca has earlier foundations, as can be seen in the sixteenth chapter of Romans, and second chapter of Acts. Women did teach and baptize. Paul never condemned women for doing so.

The most unique aspect of this story of Paul and Thelca concerns love and romance. Thelca falls in love with Paul. Paul loves Thelca. But the love that the two share is *agape* in nature—not erotic. They live in absolute continence.[6] This love affair and format of love become the hallmark of generations of later Christian love, when women renounce their families, their friends and their own physical needs to follow what is assumed to be the Christian message: one of self-denial, deprivation, abandonment, mortification of the flesh, and ultimate isolation as seen in the rise of monastic and cenobetic communities that will be scattered throughout the Christian world.

Some of the women who renounce "the world and all its ways" break away from their vows of prayer and silence and return to the world to preach and minister, as, in *Paul and Thelca*, does Artemilla, Eubulla, Numpha, Stratonike, and Theonoe. Many, such as Myrta, serve as prophets, who, in the *Didache* have the right to invoke the Eucharistic prayer, being likened to the high priests, for they are "Spirit-filled" persons. In fact, these prophetesses outranked both local priests and bishops, for only if they—or an original Apostle—were not present was a local minister, deacon, presbyter or bishop entitled to take their place.[7]

That the *Acts of Paul and Thelca* can be given credence, can be justified, and can be defended, can occur when introspecting the accepted canons of Scripture either written by Paul or a secretary of Paul, or concerning Paul, and/or the early Christian community. That women prayed at least as equals to men is the theme of Acts 1. And in Acts 1, women are ordained by the Holy Spirit to preach the Christian message "in tongues"—which must be understood as languages known to those with whom they communicated (Acts 1:14 *supra* 2:1-4). That Paul called women to the Christian message is attested in at least two places in the Acts (9:1-2, and 22:4-5). That he enjoyed the companionship of women and preached as eagerly to women as to men is demonstrated in Acts 16:13-14f. Women worked with Paul (Romans 16:3, 6, 12-15; II Tim. 4:19, 21), and some were considered Apostles (Romans

16:7), with power as great as his, as well as power and importance in the Christian community *greater* than his own (Romans 16:1-2, and Phil. 4:2-3), which even the most misogynistic Church Fathers later admitted, albeit reluctantly.[8]

Women were not only learned in the Gospel message, but preached it openly (Acts 18:24-26) more accurately than did men:

> An Alexandrian Jew named Apollos now arrived in Ephesus. He was an eloquent man, with a sound knowledge of the scriptures, and yet, though he had been given instruction in the Way of the Lord and preached with great spiritual earnestness and was accurate in all the details he taught about Jesus, he had only experienced the baptism of John. When Priscilla and Aquilla heard him speak boldly in the synagogue, they took him and expounded to him the Way of God more accurately.

The significance and value of the writer of this text putting Priscilla first, above and over her husband, did not go without notice in the early Church. No less than John Chrysostom wrote: [9]

> It is worth examining Paul's motive when he greets them, for putting Priscilla before her husband. Indeed, he did not say: "Salute Aquila and Priscilla," but rather, "Salute Priscilla and Aquila" [Romans 16:3]. He did not do so without reason: the wife must have had, I think, greater piety than her husband. This is not a simple conjecture; its confirmation is evident in the Acts. Apollos was an eloquent man, well versed in Scripture, but he knew only the baptism of John; this woman took him, instructed him in the way of God, and made him an accomplished teacher.

Paul, himself confirms the teaching prowess of women. Their knowledge and expertise is equal to that of men

(I Tim. 3:8-11; *gynaikas* must be seen in referent-comparison to vs. 1-7).[10]

If Christ, Paul, and other male Apostles, and the early Christian community could accept women on par with men in all phases and facets of society, especially in ministering of the word of God,[11] how can the contemporary twentieth century churches reject the right and God-commissioned ordained call of women to the ministry, priesthood, and episcopacy of the church? Since Paul was able to accept the rule of women over him, can the contemporary Christian do any less? Is it not time, in the Christian church, for female bishops—and, especially in the Roman Catholic church, for a female pope? I, for one, would heartily welcome both, for then the church would live up to the example and message of Christ.[12]

NOTES

[1]W.E. Thomas, "The Place of Women in the Church at Philippi," *Expository Times*, 83 (1972), pp. 117-120; R.W. Graham, "Women in the Pauline Churches: A Review Article," *Lexington Theological Quarterly*, 11 (1976), pp. 25-33; those who are considered "subordinate" are discussed in E.E. Ellis, "Paul and His Co-Workers," *New Testament Studies* 17 (1970-1971), pp. 437-452.

[2]See my *Woman as Priest, Bishop and Laity in the Early Catholic Church*.

[3]M.J. Lagrange, *Saint Paul: Épitre aux Romains* (Paris, 1916), p. 366, and my *Woman as Priest*, chap. 6.

[4]B. Bauer, "Uxores Circumducere (1 Kor. 9:5)," *Biblische Zeitschrift*, 3 (1959), pp. 94-102; A. Lemaire, "From Services to Ministries," *Concilium*, 14 (1972), pp. 35-49; J. Gnika, *Der Philipperbrief* (Freiburg: Herder, 1968), pp. 35f; G.B. Caird, "Paul and Women's Liberty," *Bulletin of the John Rylands Library*, 54 (1972), pp. 268-281; M.D. Hooker, "Authority on Her Head: An Examination of 1 Cor. 11:10," *New Testament Studies*, 10 (1963-1964), pp. 410-416; J.B. Hurley, "Did Paul Require Veils or the Silence of Women? A Consideration of 1 Cor. 11:2-16 and 1 Cor. 14:33b-36," *Westminster Theological Journal*, 35 (1972-1973), pp. 190-220; E. Kähler, *Die Frau in den Paulinischen Briefen* (Zurich: Gotthelf, 1960); S. Lösch, "Christliche Frauen

Chapter Nine
Woman, Priesthood & Gnosticism

By the second century of the current era (100-199 CE), there was a wide spread belief, originating in Asia Minor, that Jesus was never a human being. Instead, the new thought held that Jesus was a Docetic appearance—or a ghost which was visible in human form. This belief makes up much of early Gnostic thought which was unable to accept the physical degradation of Jesus with his alleged resurrection and immortality. The fact that a man from Galilee could have been pre-existent, and exist throughout eternity in a' special glory after suffering base humiliation at the hands of mortals did not appear consistant. To explain this problem in Christology, as it stood, Gnostics argued that Jesus did in fact appear on earth, and that he taught his disciples—both male and female—but never as a man, but instead as a heavenly being in mortal manifestation.

This belief, however, was neither the fullness of Gnosticism (a word meaning "to know," based on γνωσις or "knowledge"), nor its fundamental principle, during the height of its influence (135 - 160 CE), when it threatened to overwhelm historic Christianity and thus brought out a grave crisis in the established Christian church because of its insistence on the efficacy of prayers regardless of gender, its acceptance of women as equals, and its belief in "divine calling" regardless of sexuality, sexual distinction, or sexual expression. This in itself forced the "orthodox" church to pull back, reappraise, and ultimately limit and then exclude women from the heirarchy and priesthood.

True Gnosticism was to be a special knowledge that was forever mystical. This knowledge was a supernatural wisdom by which those who were to be initiated into Gnosticism, and ultimately be confirmed into the faith of the Gnostic movement were to be brought to a new and a true understanding of the universe. This understanding would come by denying the corporality of life and the elements of life, and thus when the individual eschewed mortality that individual would be saved from the evil world of matter.

Fundamental among the Gnostic thought movement was the concept and doctrine of salvation. Akin to many of the world's mystery religions at this time, Gnosticism expressed a viable and variable host of ideas gleened from numerous cults and confessions, and thus like traditional and historical Christianity became a conglomerate of philosophies and practices. Like traditional, "main-stream" Christianity, Gnosticism thrived on mystery, magic, remembrances akin to the worship of previous deities, and a priesthood. What separated it most distinctly from traditional/historical Christianity was its syncretic mixture of equality and determination.

Gnosticism, although reaching its apogee in the second century of the current era, is older than Christianity. It, like Christianity, has its roots in pre-Christian thought and practice: including special and distinct Jewish and non-Jewish pre-Christian theology and worship. It is to be found in the Hermetic literature of Egypt. It's astral elements are to be found in Babylonian religious concepts. Its dualistic concept of the universe is Persian in origin. And its primary purpose was to grasp and become a part of the emanations from God in the "pleroma" (or realm of the spirit)—a doctrine distinctly Egyptian.

Combining the Platonic theory of the contrast between the real world of spiritual spheres of ideas and the visible world of phenomena, Gnosticism added the dualism of Persian thought that there was a constant struggle between good and evil, light and darkness, where mortals struggle to obtain good and permanent spiritual (non-physical) salvation, but usually lose to a place of imprisonment which was generally believed to be within his own mind— a confining place not permitting knowledge to grow or expand. The only way a mortal could escape the prison of the flesh was to deny the flesh and work towards selflessness coupled with disinterest in material possessions or laudations by other mortals. Once freed from the bondage of the visible, corporal world, and from its rulers, the individual could join with spacial planetary rulers, and once initiated, commune with the true realm of spiritual realities.

As the world began to offer less promise and danger lurked everywhere as societies crumbled, morality was questioned, censorship of thought, word and deed increased as metaphysical speculation was either banned or limited, Gnosticism grew. With the appearance of the message of Christianity married to the individual known as Jesus, Gnosticism borrowed from its teachers while, at the same time, returning many thoughts and practices which were quickly merged into mainstream Christianity as a faith and lifestyle. For a while it was difficult to tell where one faith began and the other ended. The *persona* of Christ was easily and quickly adapted to the basic Gnostic philosophy. Jesus was seen as the "revealer" of the previously "unknown" "powerful and all-perfect godhead." Since Jesus spoke a message of faith and of love, and talked of a special mansion of many rooms, Gnostic thinkers believed that the man referred to a non-earthly paradise—more than a garden (*Gan Eden*) and close to the source of all wisdom (*haskil*).

Since the material world is evil and Jesus' message was like his "kingdom"—"not of this world" he was believed to be strictly divine and not a real incarnation. This is in keeping with many of Paul's own teachings. Paul sharply differed from the Petrine apologists, by contrasting "things of the flesh and things of the spirit" (I Cor. 2:6), and argued that Jesus was victor over those "principalities and powers" which are "world rulers of this darkness" (Col. 2:15, and Eph. 6:12). Furthermore Paul argued that Christ was from heaven (I Cor. 15:47), who would impart a special "wisdom among the perfect" (Romans 8:22-25, and I Cor. 15:50). Thus, understandably, Paul was always the "chief apostle" to the Gnostics, whereas Peter ranked first among the traditional/historic Christians.

Even though Paul was seen as "the chief apostle," his writings were not the mainstay of Gnosticism. Instead the backbone of the movement after the rise of traditional/historic Christianity came from the writings of Satornilus of Antioch.

Satornilus (or Saturninus, born in Syria sometime in the second century), was first recorded by St. Irenaeus.[1]

It has been said that Satornilus was a pupil of Menander, the student of Simon Magus, and to have taught in Antioch. He was responsible for the authorship and propagation of the thought that the origin of all things was to be sought in a Father unknown to all humankind, who created a series of angels and other supernatural beings. These angels and other supernatural beings, once enlightened from "the fountainhead of the Father" then created humankind.

Once created by the angels, man was a powerless entity who wriggled on the earth like a worm (ως σκωληκος σκαριζοντος) until a Divine spark set him on his feet. This spark was the knowledge to stand erect, an ability which he would retain provided he would reject marriage and the use of meat in his diet.[2]

About the same time as Satronilus of Antioch, Basilides taught in Alexandria, who more than likely was also Syrian born in the second century of the current era. More ambitious than most teachers of his generation , Basilides made little pretense of humility. Instead he declared that he possessed the "secret tradition" transmitted from St. Peter as to how one would be saved of ailments and sin. He taught that YHWH ("the god of the Jews") was more of an angel than the ultimate deity, and as such belonged to the lower ranks of spiritual beings. YHWH was seen as a vicious, vindictive godling who wanted to subject all mortals to his irrational, capricious and cruel will. Because this godling belonged to the lowest ranks of the angels and yet pretended to have dominion over lives and souls, the "Supreme God" sent his Nous (or, mind) into the world to free it from enslavement to YHWH.

The Nous of this Supreme Deity dwelt in Jesus. Jesus, Basilides argued, appeared in the form of a man—but that was merely a ghostlike manifestation so that mortals could best comprehend the message since the medium was critical to minor mentalities. Thus when it came for Jesus to "suffer and die" only the appearance suffered and died, while the true Christ lived on. By living on—even after the death of the flesh (an argument quickly picked up and incorporated into the theology of the Christian church)—Jesus set an example for other mortals to imitate him; the Christ example was seen as a command that man must follow Jesus to win freedom from matter and rise to the Supreme godhead.[3]

Even more important than Basilides' writings were the teaching of Valentinus, who was active in Rome from about 135 to 165 CE, and who must most assuredly be regarded as one of the most gifted thinkers of his day and of the entire century.

A native of Egypt, born in the second century, Valentinus had been a student of Theodas (who had been a student of St. Paul). He began his life as a traditional/historic Christian, but seceded from the Church when it began to oppress women and glorify adiaphora. Moving to Cyprus he began to teach in earnest, winning for himself a large following, who found peace in his concept of parallels between the world of ideas ($\pi\lambda\eta\rho\omega\mu\alpha$) and the world of phenomena ($\kappa\epsilon\nu\omega\mu\alpha$)—which he drew from Plato. The main features of his arguments are an elaborate doctrine of aeons which form a succession of pairs or *syzygies* ($\sigma\upsilon\zeta\upsilon\gamma\iota\alpha$) being a composition of cosmological opposites (*e.g.* male and female). Valentinus argued that the universe came into being through the interaction of such opposites—similar to the Hegelian doctrine of thesis and antithesis—and without the pontifications of what exactly could interact with another, save for the forces of the two interacting to be different so as to make up a common unit of oneness.

These forces, commonly translated as male and female, united, and from their union produced progeny. This progeny lived in harmony until knowledge (*Sophia*, one of the lowest aeons) became the Demiurge ($\delta\eta\mu\iota\upsilon\rho\gamma\upsilon\varsigma$, or "craftsperson"—similar to the deity of the Old Testament, although originally defined by Plato in his account of the formation of the visible world, and later by Greek Christian writers who defined it as the God-Creator of all things) was limited, and in an attempt to maintain hegemony over it earth was created. Mortal beings were placed in subjection to the limited knowledge (as seen in the first beings forbidden to eat the fruit of the "Tree of Knowledge.").[4]

The ultimate Supreme Being mourned the injustice created by the petty YHWH and determined to allow humankind the opportunity to once more become a part of the Ultimate Knowledge and thus united "Himself" with the mortal man Jesus at the time of Jesus' baptism. It was in the act of the baptism that knowledge once more came to earth, for the Supreme Being brought men the gnosis through the acceptance of the water.

Valentinus was definitely not a democrat, however, for the gnosis of the Supreme Being, he argued, was given only to the "pneumatics" (*i.e.*, the Valentinians, an order Valentinus established). Possession of this gnosis also brought with it a more full understanding of the spiritual heirarchy—

a spiritual heirarchy that was ruled without reference to gender or condition. Since traditional/historic Christians were preoccupied with gender concerns and other adiaphoric and irrelevant matters, they were considered "psychics" who preached salvation through faith and good works and yet neither had true unqualified faith and seldom practiced good works without expecting or anticipating a return, and thus were consigned to the middle realm of the Demiurge since they possessed at least a seed of spirituality. However, the majority of the people were damned to eternal perdition since they were totally engrossed in matter—things of the flesh with little concern for the world community or their immediate neighbors.[5]

And like Valentinus' concept of heaven being composed of numerous "rings" or plateaus of excellence and enlightenment, so too was his concept of hell. This theory, gleaned from the Talmud and other writings, continued long after the death of the teacher Valentinus— appearing not only as Cantos in the *Divine Comedy* of Dante, but even numerous ontological and theological speculations as late as the eighteenth century writings culminating in the *Book of Mormon*.

One of those who gravitated to the writings of Valentinus was First Reformer of the Christian Church—Marcion (born in the second century, CE, in Sinope, Asia Minor). He moved to Rome in 139 CE, joined the Roman congregation, and made a sizeable monetary contribution to its benevolent works program. He studied under the popular Gnostic, Cerdo, of Rome, and came to espouse a strong and sharp dualism within nature. He saw Jesus as a Docetic manifestation, attacked the legalism of the Old

Testament which required a debasedness of humanity because of fear of a jealous tribal god of select Semetic tribes, and proclaimed that true Christians would not only reject the Old Testament but enjoin the world to love and demonstrate mercy for all human beings. This bothered many of the emerging church fathers who began to selectivize the church, and when Marcion came out against the eating of meat, and urged all people to abstain from sexual intercourse since it only played into the hands of the tribal creator-god, he was excommunicated about 144 CE.

Feeling that the Roman church had separated itself from the teachings of Jesus and the ministry of Paul, Marcion gathered his followers into a separate church. For their use he compiled a canon of sacred books composed of the ten epistles of Paul (omitting the Pastorals), and the Gospel of Luke. He rejected any passage that implied Christ regarded the Old Testament god to be his father—or was in any way related to him. In this sense Marcion was ahead of his time, for his effort—as far as can be determined—was the first attempt to form an authoritative collection of New Testament writings.

Since Marcion admitted women to full communion, while the Roman church was beginning to place limitations on women out of fear that they would rival men, his church flourished, and by the fifth century had spread into the Orient and north to the Danube. His was an espec-ially popular church since it distinguished good from bad, and placed direct limits on quality and evil—following gnostic principles separating the god of good from the god of evil. Yet as rapidly as women had entered his church in its first days, their exodus was even faster when his associate, Severus, taught that "woman is the work of Satan.... Hence, those who consort in marriage fulfill the work of Satan."[6] Although Marcion attempted to reason that the reference was to human sexuality expressed, few women viewed the teaching in the same light, but saw it as an attack on womanhood. The Roman church made sport of it, denouncing Severus for defiling a basic "component in Creation —namely Eve"—even though such rank chauvinistic misogynism was rife throughout the orthodox church as well, coming in epistles by Ignatius to sermons by Cyprian.[7]

Soon Marcion was overwhelmed, and the teachings of Severus—which made up the *corpus* of teaching of the Marcionites organized around the condemnation of regeneration and anything which appeared to be female. In the *Acts of Thomas* "communion of the male" is tantamount to proclaiming "the power of the Most High," while woman is rifled in on as the source of evil, lust, and "works of birth and decay."[8] Even Christ is made to say that woman does not deserve life unless he makes her into a man.[9] And the kingdom of god is, according to the *Gospel of Thomas*, reserved exclusively for men. Interesting enough the fullness of this particular gospel actually encourages women "to come over and be as men"—giving reason not only for cross-dressing, but even for transsexualism: "for every woman who makes herself a man shall enter the kingdom of heaven."[10]

Those who could not change their sex physically did so metaphysically or consciously by abrogating their "femaleness"—which included adopting the habits and clothing of "sexless" beings—usually by attiring in volumnous, formless cloaks which covered the entire body from head to foot—with a small opening permitted only for the eyes. This was because the human body— especially the female body—was considered "evil" and the "instrument of lust" which would, if looked upon, generate "birth and decay."[1 1]

Women who "gave up femaleness" were permitted to be priests in the Marcionist church "since they are like sexless men—devoted to god." The *raison d'etre* for this was taken from the *Gospel of Thomas*, in which Jesus rebuked Simon Peter for demanding that Mary Magdalene leave the circle of disciples, "because women are not worthy of life." Jesus, it is recorded, declared "See, I shall lead her, so that I make her a man. That she, too, may become a living spirit, who is like you men. For every woman who makes herself a man shall enter the kingdom of heaven."[1 2]

Later Apelles, another follower of Marcion, deeply influenced by the ascetic virgin Philumene (who Tertullian called a "prophet," as well as a *"praeceptrix"* and *"magistra"*) who accompanied him on his many trips, also gave women a special role in the "ministry of the faith." So revered was Philumene, that her writings were considered "holy writings"—scriptures—not only by Apelles, but by those who followed him—including the Carpocratians who appeal to Salome, Mary Magdalene and Martha as the source and guarantors of their traditions. Women ranked high in their circles—serving not only as "ministers" but also as priests and teachers, with the middle-second century Marcellina acquiring numerous students and

international acclaim. This was in part because the Carpo-
crates taught that "righteousness of God is commmunion with
equality" as expressed by Paul in his Letter to the Galatians
(3:27f).

Epiphanes went further. Not only citing Paul's letter
to the Galatians, he declared "In that God made all things
in common forman and brought together the female with
the male in common and united all the animals likewise,
he declared righteousness to be fellowship with equality."[13]

The Roman church caught on to this declaration of
faith in equality with anything but equaminity, for the
pontiffs and preachers of this time promptly charged the
Carpocratians with promoting sexual license and practicing
sexual intercourse indiscriminately (a standard polemic of
various religious groups at odds with each other). Rome's
harsh—and quite possibly unfounded charge—found "evidence" of the corruption of the Carpocratians when their
church urged people to unite "as they will and with whom
they will"[14]—even though the injunction appears to be
directed towards brotherhood rather than any form of
sexual intercourse. But the fact that the Carpocratians
believed in equality, invited women to serve as priests,
and went against the norm as taught by the power of the
traditional/historic church was believed by those in power
to be a confession of unorthodoxy and potential dissettle-
ment leading to civil unrest and disobedience.

When those who followed Valentinian attempted to
persuade the authorities that "maleness and femaleness are
not antagonistic" to one another, but instead were comple-
mentary, the charges of "wanton abandonness" reared up

again. Women, Rome declared, were "unfit to teach" since they "are unable to rule their own lives." "Preaching is of an even higher order—a calling—which must be exercised only by those truly in charge of themselves so that they can be in charge of others." "Since woman is subject to man—as is given in the laws of both Moses and Paul--she is unable to have total charge over herself and thus must be subject to man." Never once did Rome acknowledge that it was a woman who stayed with Christ the night he was arrested, although the others fled; never once was it acknowledged that it was a woman who stayed near the tomb of Christ, and the same woman who found his body gone, visited with him when he appeared to her, and was commissioned to tell the male apostles—few of whom believed at first—that he had risen from the dead; yet, in spite of the fact that Peter denied Jesus three times, Jesus' male disciples (with the initial exception of Peter who drew a sword to defend his master) ran away when the soldiers came, and one (Thomas) doubted the message of the ressurection until he had physically placed his hands into the wounds of the man from Galilee, Rome still argued that man "is by nature superior to woman, unafraid, temperate, thinking."

To the Gnostics the claims of Rome were nonsense, for Jesus was seen as the embodiment of both maleness and femaleness, The Nous which descended into Jesus at the time of the baptism in the River Jordan was the godhead father *and* mother "of all things." The union of the masculine-feminine *persona* of god is the "spiritual marriage" Paul advocated in mortals—a prefiguration of the perfect eschatological marriage union the established church advocated but never permitted. And when the Valentinians declared that such a marriage should appear in all people at all points and stages of their life, Rome and sister cities shouted that the Gnostics were advocating dual sexuality, homosexuality, bisexuality and/or androgyny— none of which were urged by any Valentinian. Instead, they pointed out in *The Gospel of Philip* that Christ came to this planet to end the separation between female and male and unite the two genders into one—not physically but spiritually. The physical "elements" of the sexes were not only "unfit for contemplation" but without value for consideration. The godhead looks upon the individual's soul, the Valentinians continued, which has no gender—it is neither male nor female—regardless of what the body gender is. Since god looks only at the soul—which is both neutral as well as "composed of that which is maleness and that which is femaleness—the essense of all creation" humankind can do no more than imitate the *persona* and thus realize spiritual, mental, internal freedom. [15]

Because of the Gnostic insistence on the humanness of emotions, and the valuelessness of sexual identity, Marcus preached a "universal love" for all people "regardless if the hearer is female or male, male or female, for both are one in the Oneness of the Nous." To emphasize his point, a point which attracted numerous women to his message and his movement, who accepted baptism into the faith he professed, sought out instructions so that they too could preach, and received ordination from him in the work of Jesus' mission on earth, he invited women to speak the thanksgiving over the eucharistic cup of mixed wine, mixed the contents of "the women's cup" with his own cup, and prayed, "May the Spirit (*Charis*) who is before all things, who is beyond thought and description, fill your inner being and multiply in you her knowledge, sowing the mustard seed in good soil."[16]

So convinced was Marcus of the right of women to be priests and prophets that he not only spoke about the equality between the sexes at length, but ordained women without hesitation. The ordination of women was a special ceremony, complete with prayers and offerings of commissions and responsibilities. Marcus, when hands were laid upon the woman to confirm in her soul the Holy Spirit, would pray:[17]

> *I desire to make you a partner in my Grace* (Charis), *since the Father of all does hold continuously your greatness* [the angel] *before his face* [Matt. 18:10] *The place of your greatness* [the angel] *is ever in us. We must come together. First, receive from me and through me Grace. Adorn yourself as a bride who expects her bridegroom, that you may be what I am, and I what you are. Receive in your bride-chamber the seed of light. Receive from me the bridegroom, and give him a place, and have a place in him. Behold Grace has descended upon you. Open your mouth and prophesy.*

Although Irenaeus made sport of the ordination ceremony, and declared it was a subtle ruse to deceive wealthy women of high social position out of both property and their physical/sexual self-respect, his condemnations must be understood as symbolic of the writings of a sexually frustrated eschatological illiterate. Irenaeus neither understood the metaphoric use of the term "the mystery of union" which his own faith declared at the point of transubstantiation, nor the purpose and intent of the words "bride," "groom," or bridechamber"— words and terms used even within his own theological community when it initiated young women into convent life and took young boys into monasteries.

The base chauvinism of Irenaeus' phobia against the Gnostics in this regard is two-fold. First, he did not understand the rite itself. Second, he based his accusations concerning the rite allegedly being a "sexual coverup" on a misunderstanding or deliberate ignorance of the *Osculum Pacis*—the "Holy Kiss" as defined in *The Gospel of Philip*. Not only was the kiss considered a greeting of peace between two people—as was to have been exchanged between Jesus and Judas Iscariot on the night the Galilean was betrayed— but it was also symbolic of pure thought and deed: "For the perfect conceive through a kiss and give birth. Because of this we also kiss each other. We receive [spiritual] conception from the Grace [of God] (*Charis*) which is among us."[18]

The act itself deserves scrutiny, for in it contains the seed elements of the faith of the Gnostics. The first sentence is an introduction into the community of believers where the "feminine principle" is both annihilated and destroyed so that it can merge into Oneness which is symbolized as "the angel" — which is greater than a mortal.

While the original text uses the words "angel," it must be read metaphorically, since "angels" were considered lesser "beings" or manifestations of the Supreme God-manifestations of power and principle, like the petty deity YHWH. This is defined in the first line, where the woman about to be ordained a prophet is told that she is to receive the grace of "the Father." This "grace" is a special selection, a putting apart from the common individuals who are still wedded to the finiteness of the earth and mortal passions. With "the grace"—or *Charis*—of the deity, the woman becomes like the angels (Ps. 8:6). This "becoming" is introduced by the woman's recognition that there is a common bond between people—she is to receive the grace through the manifestations of religious beings—the "me" being vague—being neither the officiant or the angel, but only granted through them as vicars for the Supreme Being.

Blessed with grace the woman then is to consider herself a bride. She has put the "grace" of the Supreme Being on carefully, deliberately, pain-stakingly, thoughtfully as a new bride would attire herself in her bridal clothing. The Supreme Being is her groom, and he will know that she is totally "his" (the Supreme Being, although referred to in masculine terms is, as explained by Valentinian and Marcion, gender-free) when she appears before him dressed with the special marking of "grace"—the finality of the ordination to the rank and position of prophet.

The "bride chamber" is the new prophetess' mind. In her mind she will aquire knowledge (*gnos*) of the Supreme Being (*Nous*). Committed to knowledge she will become free, and she will be able not only to understand "the secrets" of the "unknown," but will be able to intelligently and articulately explain these "secrets" to others. Many of the "sharings" of these consecrated women will be prophecies of what will happen, but since each individually consecrated woman has to learn them through a special, personal "enlightenment"—since they exist in the ultimate reality of the Nous, each woman ordained will be but mapping a course for others to better understand them, prepare themselves for what will be, and participate in the celebration of learning.

Each new prophetess will receive the Supreme Being in a manner identical to that experienced by the man from Galilee when he was baptized in the River Jordan by John, and once "grace has descended upon" her, she will by choice, inclination, determination, and decision "open" her "mouth and prophesy." This is identical to the same commission, ordination, and declaration of the early Roman church when Phoebe was a priestess for Jesus (Romans 16:16), and who, like Aquila and Priscilla worked hard for the church (quibus non solu ego gratias ago sed et cunctae ecclesiae gentium) as ministrae ad Deos. One must not ignore Acts 1:14 and 2:1-4, which specifically spells out that Christian women were to take on the duties of prophecy, and that Jesus himself demanded that women be allowed to prophesy—as recounted in Acts 2:16-18:

αλλε τουτο εστι το ειρημενον δια του προφητου Ἰωηλ
Και εσται εν ταις εσχαταις ημεραις λεγει ο Θεος
εκχεω απο του Πνευματος μου επι πασαν σαρκα και
προφητευσουσιν οι υιοι υμων και ει θυγατερες υμων
και οι νεανισκοι υμων ορασεις οψονται και οι

πρεσβυτεροι υμων ενυπνιοις ενυπνιασθησονται και
γε επι τους δουλους μου και επι τας δουλας μου εν
ταις ημεραις εκειναις εκχεω απο του Πνευματος
μου και προφητευσουσι

It is at this point that the *Osculum* (kiss) is bestowed,
as it was often given to Mary Magdalene by Jesus since
she had more fully accepted him than did his male apostles.
It is for this reason that the same Gospel reads that Jesus
loved her "more than the [other] disciples, and kissed
her on her [mouth] often."[19]

Although at first appearance it might be said that
Gnosticism was against women, it is quite the opposite.
Gnosticism turned to women as towards completion of
the unification of *syzygies*—or couples necessary to complete the plan of the Supreme Being. What Gnosticism
was against was "feminine principle" or "feminism" as
a characteristic which had, because of generations-long
conditioning, forced women to believe, accept, and act
out the role of being "less than men, weaker than men,
subject to men, and needing men." Far from being a
chauvinistic theology, Gnosticism was antithetical to
misogynism in thought, theology, and deed; it heralded
the "rebirth of women as men"—not by demanding that
women give up being women, but rather insisting that
women become aggressive, assertive, determined, self-
actualized, strengthened, resolute, and participative with
men in all things on par with men as true equals. "Maleness," which many opponents of Gnosticism have attacked
as being chauvinistic, and argued that the Gnostics saw
men as "virile," "strong and resolute," "divine and absolute"

in all things, saw only the words on parchment—they did not read the context of the written page. Instead of their being a glorification of "men" as a gender, such as was done by Clement of Alexandria and other chauvinists who filled the Roman church, the ancient Gnostics lauded "masculine principle": the "maleness" of resolve, strength, determination, standfastness, purpose, independence, and assertiveness- that which is "strong" in any terminology. "Maleness" was overcoming the selfishness of pettiness as demonstrated by YHWH who created a special realm over which that godling could terrorize, intimidate, and frighten mortals. "Maleness" was the purpose of escaping into selflessness, merging into Oneness with Knowledge, the Essense of the Supreme Being, and being freed from all corporal, mortal, and perishable realms of reality— mental or physical.

The dualism of Gnosticism reflects the chasm between the world divine and the world temporal. It separates the carnal flesh from the immortal soul. But in order to express it so that those less philosophically oriented could understand the principles of this ontology, simple, identifiable words were used: with the most common words "male" and "female" employed in their accepted context of understanding to define "strength" (male), and "weakness" (female). Once women understood this definition and usage of words and terms centered around gender description, those that were willing to overthrow convention, centuries of tradition which blocked their advance to human and intellectual freedom, returned to the Gnostic fold and entered into communion with its congregants—many becoming ordained to the Gnostic priesthood.

Gnosticism followed the embryonic Christian church. It appealed to apostolic revelation and nonsexist tradition to justify its order and theology. It separated from the traditional/historic Christian church by rejecting patriarchalism that slowly inched its way into the Christian community on the spurious grounds that allegedly an apostle had ruled against women speaking in a congregation of believers—or performing any "apostolic function." The often quoted line of Paul's rejection of women preaching, was in fact intensified and increased in venomous augmentation by the gynophobe Tertullian in an exegesis—an exegetical writing rejected by the Gnostics as an overinterpolation of an apocryphal writing which was not incorporated into their canon of scripture.[20] The ministry of women in the Gnostic church was faithfully defended not only on the basis of Paul's salutation of women who "worked for the lord" as his "equal" (Romans 16), but upon the critical account of women serving as priests in the record *The Acts of Thelca*—a scripture considered authentic and canonical not only by the Gnostics, but also by the historic Roman church.

Citing the four Gospels, the Gnostics pointed out that women were essential to Jesus and a part of his ministry from the beginning to the end. Whereas the male apostles demonstrated skepticism concerning Jesus' rising from the dead, the women did not. The male apostles did not accept the testimony of the women that Christ had indeed returned from the grave—a primary ingredient in orthodox Christianity—until the Galilean appeared before them—accompanied by a woman.[21]

While the first male apostles of Jesus were twelve in number, the Galilean's female apostles numbered seven— a number holy in all Semetic traditions and faiths. This special number was considered holy, ordained, and even predetermined as a special mark of grace from god to the world—a point not lost on the Gnostic community. It is on the basis of this holy number and the important roles played by women in the life and ministry of women that the Gnostic community emphasized the special spiritual function. This function was strengthened with reference to *The Gospel of Mary*, which resolutely declared that anyone who rejects the revelations and traditions transmitted by a woman, or under the name of a woman, rejects the true revelations of Jesus himself and forfeits eternal salvation.[22]

Uniquely the writings of the Gnostics on women, including the writings of Gnostic women on women, frightened the Roman clergy moreso than did the secular arm of the non-Christian state. Polemics were written attacking the majority of the writings, and when orthodox Christianity came into its own as the State Religion, its leaders, in true Falwellian spirit, rushed to destroy those letters which "offended the faith." It was especially essential to destroy those writings which glorified the weak (women) who would inherit the kingdom of god, while (rich) men would have a more difficult time. Even in such literature as the *Questions of Bartholomew*, a woman (Mary) is detailed as raising her hands up to the heavens in prayer—a characteristic of male priests—after having laid (reclined on a couch) with Christ at the Last Supper. The apostolic authority of women is championed by parading Galatians 3:28, and detailing the rights and roles of women in Paul's letter to the churches of Rome.

Many of the advocates for women's right to the ministry and ordination were women. This spurred on the primary opposition who sought a fundamental change in the original commission. Mincing menacingly towards women, Rome's rankest misogynist, Origen--who had such a difficult time accepting his own sexuality to the point that he emasculated himself—acknowledged the existence of Phoebe. But, belieing his own fear of being supplanted by a woman of equality, Origen reduced Phoebe to the role of being Paul's assistant and servant, never once acknowledging that in this sense and terminology a "servant" is also a "minister."[23] Chrysostom, whose own "best-friend and mentor" was a woman, accepts the fact that women were priests in the early church—in its first days—but then says without any sound reasoning that this state for women passed when the "angelic condition" ceased—implying indirectly that the emerging church was without the grace of the Holy Ghost—a comment anathematized by the Gnostic community.[24] Chrysostom, in reality, said that the nascent community had been forsaken by the godhead, and that the Christians as a people were now mere wanderers killing time until the *Nous* returned.

NOTES

[1] Irenaeus, *Haèr.* I, 22. Cp. Hippolytus, *Philosoph.* VII:28; Tertullian, *Praescr.* 3; Epiphanius, *Haer* 23. Cf. R. Liechtenhan, "Satornil," in *Realencyklopaedie fuer protestantische Theologie und Kirche* (begruendet von J.J. Herzog, . ed. 3 by A. Hauck (21 vols., 1898-1908 + Register, 1909, and Ergaenzungen und Nachtraege, 2 vols., 1913) vol. 17, (1906), p. 491f. Also, G. Bardy, "Satronil," in *Dictionnaire de Theologie Catholique*, ed. A. Vacant, E. Mangenot, and E. Amann (15 vols., 1903-1950) vol. 14, (pt. 1, 1939), col. 1310f.

[2] In many ways this idea is similar to that espoused by the Ophites, an early Gnostic sect whose opposition to YHWH led them to glorify his opponent, the serpent, as the Liberator and Illuminator of humankind since it was the serpent who dialogued with "Eve" and wished to give knowledge to the early humans in Eden. This doctrine was also expressed by the Naassenes, a branch of the Ophites, and by the Cainites and Sethites. See, R.A. Lipsius, "Ueber die ophitischen Systeme," in *Zeitschrift fuer wissenschaftliche Theologie* 6(1863), pp. 410-457, and E. Amann, "Ophites" in *Dictionnaire de Theologie Catholique* 9 (pt. 1, 1931), cols. 1063-1075. See my *The Early Gnostic Movement* (Whitewater: Universitatis, 1974), pp. 321-389., with the texts in translation in part in W. Voelker, *Quellen zur Geschichte der christlichen Gnosis* (Sammlung ausgewaehlter kirchen- und dogmengeschichtliche Quellenschriften, F.F., v; 1932), pp. 11-27, from Hippolytus' canons compiled approximately 500 CE, in Greek originally, but then lost. The actual canons survive in Arabic and Ethiopic versions of a Coptic translation, probably recorded in the thirteenth century. Consult D.B. von Haneberg's edition (1870) which gives the Arabic along with a Latin translation. I used the Arabic edition, with detailed commentary on why I do not agree with the conclusions of R.H. Connolly and E. Schwartz on their historical position and importance.

[3] Authoring over 30 works, including a Gospel, Basilides works today are lost. None of his contemporaries agree on his teachings as to extent, importance, subject matter or the like, with the most critical comments coming from the primary fathers of basic orthodoxy (Irenaeus, *Adv. Haer.* 1:24; Clement of Alexandria, *Stromata*, passim). See P.J.G.A. Hendrix, *De Alexandrijnsche Haeresiarch Basilides* (Amsterdam, 1926).

[4] Iranaeus, *Adv. Haer.*, 1, passim, and 3:4; Tertullian, *Adv. Valentinianos*; Clement of Alexandria, *Stromateis* has several references; Epiphanius, *Haer.*, 31, 33. Some fragments of Valentinius' works have been assembled in A. Hilgenfeld, *Die Ketzergeschichte des Urchristenthums* (1884): pp. 283-316, 461-522. Some fragments are set in W. Voelker, *Quellen zur Geschichte der christlichen Gnosis* (1932), pp. 57-141, with the most comprehensive study being offered by F.M.M. Sagnard, O.P., *La Gnose valentinienne et le témoignage de saint Irénée* (Etudes de Philosophie médiévale, 37, 1947). Numerous articles have appeared, with an outstanding contribution offered by R.A. Lipsius, "Valentinus und seine Schule" in *Jahrbuecher fuer protestantishce Theologie* (1887), pp. 585-658. The popularity of Valentinus can be found in Tertullian's *Adv. Valentin.*, 1, when he writes *"frequentissimum collegium inter haereticos."* Cp., G. Quispel, "The Original Doctrine of Valentine," in *Vigilae Christianae* 1 (1947) pp. 43-73. On the issue of the "Tree of Life" and the role of the Serpent in the Quest for Knowledge, see my *Woman in Ancient Israel Under the Torah and the Talmud; with a Parallel Translation and Critical Commentary on Genesis 1-3* (Mesquite, 1980).

[5] Cf. O. Dibelius, "Studien zur Geschichte der Valentinianer," in *Zeitschrift fuer die neutestamentliche Wissenschaft und die Kunde des Urchristentums* 6 (Giessen, 1908) pp. 237-247, 329-340. C. Barth, *Die Interpretation des Neuen Testaments in der valentinianischen Gnosis* as a part of *Texte und Untersuchungen zur Geschichte der altchristlichen literatur*, begrundet

von O. von Gebhardt und A. Harnach, (Leipzig, 1882ff) 37 (Hft. 3; 1911).

[6]Epiphanius, *Panarion*, XLV, 2:1. See my *Misogynism in the Early Gnostic Community and the Response of Valentinus* (Toronto: Theologie, 1982).

[7]R.A. Baer, *Philo's Use of the Categories of Male and Female* (Leiden: E.J. Brill, 1970), pp. 65-80. On the Gnostic teachings of Marcion, see H. Jonas, *The Gnostic Religion: The Message of the Alien God and the Beginnings of Christianity* (2d. ed., enlarged, Boston: Beacon Press, 1963), pp. 236ff. See also my *Woman in the Early Gnostic Church* (as cited).

[8]*Gospel of the Egyptians*, in *New Testament Apocrypha*, ed. Hennecke and Schneemelcher (Philadelphia: Westminster, 1965) I, pp. 166ff.

[9]Acts of Thomas 27. Cp. Pseudo-Clementines, *Homilies* II:15.3, with critical commentary offered by G. Strecker, *Das Judenchristentum in den Pseudo-klementinen* (Gottingen, 1958), pp. 35-96, and J. Jervell, *Imago Dei: Gn 1, 26f. im Spatjudentum, in der Gnosis und in den Paulinischen Briefen* (Goettingen: Vandenhoeck & Ruprecht, 1960), pp. 163.

[10]*Gospel of Thomas*, Log. 114.For a critique, see B. Gaertner, *The Theology of the Gospel of Thomas* (London: Collins, 1961). On the issue of man-woman relationships in the Gnostic system as based on the *Gospel of Thomas*, see pp. 253f.

[11]*Gospel of the Egyptians*. See my *Commentary on the Gospel of the Egyptians and the Early Gnostic Attitude Towards Women* (Toronto, 1975).

[12]*Gospel of Thomas*, Log. 114, see my *Teachings of Jesus on Women* (Dallas: Texas Independent Press, 1984).

[13]Clement of Alexandria, *Stromateis*, II, 2, no. 6.

[14]*Ibid.*, no. 10:1. See other objections in Tertullian, *Adv. Marcionem* III:11, and his *De Praescr. Haer.*, 30:6. On the Carpocratians, see H. Kraft, "Gab es einen Gnostiker Karpokrates?" in *Theologische Zeitschrift*, 8 (1952) pp. 434-443. See my *Woman in the Early Gnostic Church* for additional commentary.

[15]R. McL. Wilson, *The Gospel of Philip* (London: Mowbray, 1962) 71.

[16]Irenaeus, *Adv. Haer.*, I:13.2.

[17]*Ibid.*, 14:1.

[18]*Gospel of Philip* 31.

[19]*Ibid.*, 32, 35. The kiss has been a historic experience. See F.L. Ganshoff, *Feudalism*, for a introduction. See my *The Kiss in History and Theology* (London and Sidney, 1981).

[20]Tertullian, *De Virginibus Velandis*, IX. Cf. Ch. Stuecklin, *Tertullian, De virginibus velandis* (Bern: H. Lang, 1974), pp. 189-203.

[21]See my *Jews, Jesus & Woman in the Early Apostolic Age* (Mesquite, 1984). Cp. Luke 24:11 for the basic foundation for misinterpolation, whereas rather than it being a condemnation of women bringing the message of the resurrection to the male followers of the man from Galilee, the actual text declares that it was the men who would not receive it. The misogynistic skepticism of the male apostles was enhanced with a further treatment in the *Epistula Apostolorum*, an apocryphal document dating from the second century ("Testament of Our Lord in Galilee"), which was written in the form of an encyclical and sent out by the eleven male apostles after the resurrection. Although it was originally written in Greek, today it survives only in Ethiopic, Coptic (although incomplete), and in a single leaf in Latin. A polemic, it was written as an attack against the Gnostics, emanating from either Asia Minor or Egypt. See C. Schmidt, *Gespraeche Jesu mit seinen Juengern nach der Auferstehung* in *Texte und Untersuchungen zur Geschichte der altchristlichen Literatur* (as cited) 43 (1919). Several articles have been written by I. Delazer, O.F.M., including, "Disquisito in Argumentum Epistolae Apostolorum," in *Antonianum* 3 (1928) pp. 369-403, and "De Tempore Compositionis Epistolae Apostolorum," *ibid.*, 4 (1929) pp. 257-292 and 387-430.

[22]Gospel of Mary, published in W.C. Till, *Die gnostischen Schrfiten des koptischen Papyrus Berolinensis* (Berlin: Akademie Verlag, 1955), pp. 68-72.

[23]Origen, *Rom.* 10:17, in J.-P. Migne, *Patrologia...Graeca* vol. 14, cols. 1278A-C.

[24]E.A. Clark, "Sexual Politics in the Writings of John Chrysostom," *Anglican Theological Review*, 59 (1977), pp. 3-20. See my *Woman and John Chrysostom* (San Diego, 1976). The issue of human sexuality and religion is growing in importance. See D.F. Winslow, "Priesthood and Sexuality in the Post-Nicene Fathers," in *The Saint Luke Journal of Theology* 18 (1975), pp. 214-227, and my *Sex, Woman & Religion* (Dallas: Monument Press, 1985), and *Loving Women: A Study of Lesbianism to 500 CE* (Arlington: Liberal Arts, 1985), which gives a side to history and theology that most theologians, especially males, choose to ignore or discredit.

INDEX